# Super Easy Juicing for Beginners

1700 Days of Fresh, Invigorating Recipes for Optimal Wellness, Natural Detoxification, and Sustained Energy - Transform Your Health, One Juice at a Time

*Clara Pennington*

© Copyright 2024 by Clara Pennington- All rights reserved. The following Book is reproduced below with the goal of providing information that is as accurate and reliable as possible. Regardless, purchasing this Book can be seen as consent to the fact that both the publisher and the author of this book are in no way experts on the topics discussed within and that any recommendations or suggestions that are made herein are for entertainment purposes only. Professionals should be consulted as needed prior to undertaking any of the action endorsed herein. This declaration is deemed fair and valid by both the American Bar Association and the Committee of Publishers Association and is legally binding throughout the United States. Furthermore, the transmission, duplication, or reproduction of any of the following work including specific information will be considered an illegal act irrespective of if it is done electronically or in print. This extends to creating a secondary or tertiary copy of the work or a recorded copy and is only allowed with the express written consent from the Publisher. All additional right reserved. The information in the following pages is broadly considered a truthful and accurate account of facts and as such, any inattention, use, or misuse of the information in question by the reader will render any resulting actions solely under their purview. There are no scenarios in which the publisher or the original author of this work can be in any fashion deemed liable for any hardship or damages that may befall them after undertaking information described herein. Additionally, the information in the following pages is intended only for informational purposes and should thus be thought of as universal. As befitting its nature, it is presented without assurance regarding its prolonged validity or interim quality. Trademarks that are mentioned are done without written consent and can in no way be considered an endorsement from the trademark holder.

# Table of Contents

## 1. WELCOME TO JUICING: A NEWCOMER'S GUIDE .............................................. 13
- Introduction to Juicing ..................................................................................... 13
- Understanding the Basics ............................................................................... 15
- Setting Up Your Juicing Space ........................................................................ 16
- Tips for Juicing Success .................................................................................. 18

## 2. UNVEILING THE HEALTH ADVANTAGES OF JUICING ................................. 20
- Nutritional Benefits of Juicing ........................................................................ 20
- Enhancing Digestive Health ........................................................................... 22
- Boosting Immunity and Energy ..................................................................... 24
- Detoxification and Weight Management ...................................................... 25

## 3. PREPARING YOUR PRODUCE: BEST PRACTICES ........................................ 27
- Selecting Quality Fruits and Vegetables ....................................................... 27
- Cleaning and Prepping Techniques ............................................................... 29
- The Importance of Organic Produce .............................................................. 31
- Storing Your Ingredients for Freshness ........................................................ 32

## 4. DIVERSIFYING YOUR JUICING EXPERIENCE .............................................. 34
- Exploring Additives and Superfoods ............................................................. 34
- Balancing Flavors ............................................................................................ 36
- Creative Combinations ................................................................................... 37
- Experimenting with Herbs and Spices .......................................................... 38

## 5. CRAFTING FRUIT-CENTRIC JUICES ............................................................. 40
- Sweet and Tangy Recipes ............................................................................... 40
  - *Recipe 1: Mango Tango Citrus Blast* ........................................................ *40*
  - *Recipe 2: Strawberry Lemonade Zing* ...................................................... *40*
  - *Recipe 3: Pineapple Ginger Spark* ............................................................ *40*
  - *Recipe 4: Blueberry Pomegranate Bliss* ................................................... *41*
  - *Recipe 5: Kiwi Cucumber Cooler* .............................................................. *41*
  - *Recipe 6: Raspberry Lime Rickey* ............................................................. *41*
  - *Recipe 7: Citrus Burst Sunshine* ............................................................... *41*

*Recipe 8: Watermelon Lemonade* .................................................................................. *42*

*Recipe 9: Peachy Keen Ginger Squeeze* ....................................................................... *42*

*Recipe 10: Tart Cherry Elixir* ......................................................................................... *42*

SEASONAL FRUIT JUICES ..................................................................................................... 43

*Recipe 1: Green Goddess Revival* ................................................................................. *43*

*Recipe 2: Autumn Apple Spice* ..................................................................................... *43*

*Recipe 3: Tropical Winter Boost* ................................................................................... *44*

*Recipe 4: Spring Melody* ................................................................................................ *44*

*Recipe 5: Early Summer Peach Splash* ........................................................................ *44*

*Recipe 6: Late Summer Watermelon Wave* ................................................................ *44*

*Recipe 7: Fall Pomegranate Passion* ............................................................................ *45*

*Recipe 8: Winter Citrus Blast* ........................................................................................ *45*

*Recipe 9: Spring Green Reviver* .................................................................................... *45*

*Recipe 10: Sunny Citrus Cooler* .................................................................................... *45*

CITRUS BLENDS .................................................................................................................... 46

*Recipe 1: Sunrise Citrus Symphony* .............................................................................. *46*

*Recipe 2: Citrus Zest Cooler* .......................................................................................... *46*

*Recipe 3: Tropical Citrus Blast* ...................................................................................... *47*

*Recipe 4: Lemon Lime Fusion* ....................................................................................... *47*

*Recipe 5: Citrus Ginger Spark* ....................................................................................... *47*

*Recipe 6: Sweet Citrus Surprise* .................................................................................... *48*

*Recipe 7: Citrus Mint Refresh* ....................................................................................... *48*

*Recipe 8: Spicy Citrus Wake-Up* ................................................................................... *49*

*Recipe 9: Citrus Beet Elixir* ........................................................................................... *49*

*Recipe 10: Green Citrus Twist* ...................................................................................... *49*

EXOTIC FRUIT COMBINATIONS ........................................................................................... 50

*Recipe 1: Dragonfruit Delight* ....................................................................................... *50*

*Recipe 2: Passionate Mango Tango* ............................................................................. *50*

*Recipe 3: Kiwi Quencher* ................................................................................................ *51*

*Recipe 4: Tropical Berry Bliss* ....................................................................................... *51*

*Recipe 5: Guava Glow* .................................................................................................... *51*

*Recipe 6: Lychee Lush* .................................................................................................... *51*

*Recipe 7: Pomegranate Persuasion* .............................................................................. *52*

*Recipe 8: Soursop Serenity* ............................................................................................................. *52*

*Recipe 9: Carambola Citrus Splash* ................................................................................................ *52*

## 6. DELVING INTO VEGETABLE JUICES ................................................................................. 53

### Leafy Greens and Their Benefits ................................................................................................ 53

*Recipe 1: Kale and Spinach Elixir* ................................................................................................... *53*

*Recipe 2: Celery Cilantro Cleanse* .................................................................................................. *53*

*Recipe 3: Minty Pea Shoot Drink* .................................................................................................... *54*

*Recipe 4: Swiss Chard Citrus Boost* ................................................................................................ *54*

*Recipe 5: Collard Green Pineapple Zest* ......................................................................................... *54*

*Recipe 6: Arugula Apple Tango* ....................................................................................................... *55*

*Recipe 7: Mustard Greens Melody* ................................................................................................... *55*

*Recipe 8: Beet Greens and Berry* ..................................................................................................... *55*

*Recipe 9: Dandelion Detox Delight* .................................................................................................. *56*

*Recipe 10: Watercress Wellness Wave* ............................................................................................. *56*

### Root Vegetable Recipes ................................................................................................................. 57

*Recipe 1: Carrot Ginger Glow* .......................................................................................................... *57*

*Recipe 2: Beetroot and Apple Bliss* .................................................................................................. *57*

*Recipe 3: Sweet Potato Sunrise* ........................................................................................................ *58*

*Recipe 4: Turnip Twister* ................................................................................................................... *58*

*Recipe 5: Radish Refresher* ............................................................................................................... *58*

*Recipe 6: Parsnip Pear Potion* .......................................................................................................... *59*

*Recipe 7: Spicy Gingered Carrot* ...................................................................................................... *59*

*Recipe 8: Celery Root Citrus Blast* ................................................................................................... *59*

*Recipe 9: Golden Beet Elixir* ............................................................................................................. *60*

### Nightshade Vegetable Juices ........................................................................................................ 60

*Recipe 1: Tomato Tango Detox* ......................................................................................................... *60*

*Recipe 2: Spicy Eggplant Elixir* ........................................................................................................ *61*

*Recipe 3: Peppery Potato Punch* ....................................................................................................... *61*

*Recipe 4: Chili Pepper Power Shot* ................................................................................................... *61*

*Recipe 5: Bell Pepper Bliss* ............................................................................................................... *62*

*Recipe 6: Solanum Smoothie* ............................................................................................................. *62*

*Recipe 7: Tomatillo Twist* .................................................................................................................. *62*

*Recipe 8: Savory Solanaceae Squeeze* ............................................................................................. *63*

- *Recipe 9: Aubergine Dream* .................................................................................................. 63
- *Recipe 10: Daikon Digestive Tonic* ....................................................................................... 64

## BITTER AND SAVORY OPTIONS .................................................................................................. 64

- *Recipe 1: Bitter Greens Tonic* ................................................................................................. 64
- *Recipe 2: Savory Beet Broth* ................................................................................................... 65
- *Recipe 3: Cabbage Cure* .......................................................................................................... 65
- *Recipe 4: Fennel Freshness* .................................................................................................... 65
- *Recipe 5: Bitter Melon Magic* ................................................................................................. 66
- *Recipe 6: Savory Tomato Sip* .................................................................................................. 66
- *Recipe 7: Kale and Kombu Drink* ........................................................................................... 66
- *Recipe 8: Radish Detoxifier* .................................................................................................... 67
- *Recipe 9: Gingered Greens* ..................................................................................................... 67

# 7. THE WORLD OF SMOOTHIES ........................................................................... 68

## BASIC SMOOTHIE BUILDING BLOCKS ......................................................................................... 68

- *Recipe 1: Classic Berry Banana Smoothie* ............................................................................. 68
- *Recipe 2: Green Power Smoothie* ........................................................................................... 68
- *Recipe 3: Tropical Mango Sunrise* ......................................................................................... 68
- *Recipe 4: Peanut Butter Banana Protein* ............................................................................... 69
- *Recipe 5: Antioxidant Acai Bowl* ............................................................................................ 69
- *Recipe 6: Chocolate Avocado Bliss* ........................................................................................ 69
- *Recipe 7: Oatmeal Breakfast Smoothie* .................................................................................. 70
- *Recipe 8: Super Seed Smoothie* .............................................................................................. 70
- *Recipe 9: Detox Green Machine* ............................................................................................. 70

## PROTEIN-PACKED RECIPES ......................................................................................................... 71

- *Recipe 1: Vanilla Almond Protein Shake* ............................................................................... 71
- *Recipe 2: Berry Spinach Power Smoothie* .............................................................................. 71
- *Recipe 3: Spinach Avocado Protein Smoothie* ....................................................................... 72
- *Recipe 4: Mocha Morning Boost* ............................................................................................ 72
- *Recipe 5: Tropical Hemp Seed Smoothie* ............................................................................... 73
- *Recipe 6: Almond Joy Protein Shake* ..................................................................................... 73
- *Recipe 7: Pumpkin Pie Protein Smoothie* .............................................................................. 73
- *Recipe 8: Blueberry Oatmeal Protein Smoothie* .................................................................... 74
- *Recipe 9: Apple Cinnamon Protein Smoothie* ....................................................................... 74

Breakfast Smoothie Ideas ............................................................................................... 75
   *Recipe 1: Sunrise Berry Oat Smoothie* ................................................................. 75
   *Recipe 2: Green Protein Power Smoothie* ............................................................ 75
   *Recipe 3: Nutty Banana Flax Smoothie* ............................................................... 76
   *Recipe 4: Tropical Mango Coconut Smoothie* ..................................................... 76
   *Recipe 5: Berry Beet Detox Smoothie* .................................................................. 76
   *Recipe 6: Peanut Butter Oatmeal Smoothie* ........................................................ 77
   *Recipe 7: Kale Pineapple Ginger Smoothie* ........................................................ 77
   *Recipe 8: Chocolate Avocado Smoothie* ............................................................. 77
   *Recipe 9: Apple Pie Smoothie* ............................................................................. 78

Dessert-Inspired Creations .......................................................................................... 78
   *Recipe 1: Chocolate Hazelnut Heaven* ................................................................ 78
   *Recipe 2: Key Lime Pie Smoothie* ....................................................................... 79
   *Recipe 3: Apple Crisp Smoothie* .......................................................................... 79
   *Recipe 4: Pumpkin Spice Latte Smoothie* ........................................................... 79
   *Recipe 5: Blueberry Cheesecake Smoothie* ........................................................ 80
   *Recipe 6: Peanut Butter Cup Smoothie* .............................................................. 80
   *Recipe 7: Strawberry Shortcake Smoothie* ......................................................... 80
   *Recipe 8: Banana Cream Pie Smoothie* .............................................................. 81
   *Recipe 9: Carrot Cake Smoothie* ......................................................................... 81
   *Recipe 10: Mojito-Inspired Minty Lime Smoothie* ............................................. 82

## 8. FUSION JUICES: THE BEST OF BOTH WORLDS ................................................ 83

Fruit and Vegetable Blends .......................................................................................... 83
   *Recipe 1: Sunrise Citrus Beet* .............................................................................. 83
   *Recipe 2: Green Pineapple Bliss* ......................................................................... 83
   *Recipe 3: Carrot Apple Zinger* ............................................................................ 83
   *Recipe 4: Berry Spinach Delight* ......................................................................... 84
   *Recipe 5: Tropical Turmeric Cleanser* ................................................................ 84
   *Recipe 6: Cucumber Melon Hydrator* ................................................................ 85
   *Recipe 7: Sweet Potato Sunrise* .......................................................................... 85
   *Recipe 8: Beetroot Berry Fusion* ......................................................................... 85
   *Recipe 9: Celery Pear Cleanse* ............................................................................ 86

Tropical Mixes ............................................................................................................... 86

*Recipe 1: Mango Passion Fruit Bliss* ...... 86
*Recipe 2: Pineapple Coconut Hydrator* ...... 86
*Recipe 3: Kiwi Cucumber Cooler* ...... 87
*Recipe 4: Tropical Turmeric Tonic* ...... 87
*Recipe 5: Caribbean Citrus Burst* ...... 88
*Recipe 6: Banana Berry Lagoon* ...... 88
*Recipe 7: Avocado Lime Smoothie* ...... 88
*Recipe 8: Papaya Ginger Sunrise* ...... 89
*Recipe 9: Dragon Fruit Dream* ...... 89

ANTIOXIDANT-RICH COMBINATIONS ...... 90
*Recipe 1: Berry Beet Bliss* ...... 90
*Recipe 2: Green Tea Citrus Twist* ...... 90
*Recipe 3: Pomegranate Blueberry Punch* ...... 90
*Recipe 4: Carrot Ginger Turmeric Elixir* ...... 91
*Recipe 5: Spinach Kiwi Cooler* ...... 91
*Recipe 6: Watermelon Basil Quencher* ...... 91
*Recipe 7: Cranberry Apple Zest* ...... 92
*Recipe 8: Cherry Almond Antioxidant Smoothie* ...... 92
*Recipe 9: Sweet Potato Sunrise* ...... 93

REFRESHING HYDRATION JUICES ...... 93
*Recipe 1: Cucumber Mint Refresher* ...... 93
*Recipe 2: Watermelon Basil Bliss* ...... 93
*Recipe 3: Pineapple Coconut Hydrator* ...... 94
*Recipe 4: Green Apple Hydration* ...... 94
*Recipe 5: Berry Citrus Splash* ...... 94
*Recipe 6: Ginger Peach Quencher* ...... 95
*Recipe 7: Citrus Cucumber Cooler* ...... 95
*Recipe 8: Melon Mint Medley* ...... 95
*Recipe 9: Tropical Green Hydration* ...... 96

## 9. YOUR 21-DAY JUICE CLEANSE ...... 97

WEEK 1 ...... 97
WEEK 2 ...... 98
WEEK 3 ...... 99

**APPENDIX** .................................................................................................. **100**
- Juicing Glossary ........................................................................................ 100
- Frequently Asked Questions ................................................................... 102
- Resource Guide ......................................................................................... 104
- Index ........................................................................................................... 106

**MEASUREMENT CONVERSION TABLE** ................................................................ **107**

# 1. Welcome to Juicing: A Newcomer's Guide

## Introduction to Juicing

Embarking on a juicing journey ushers in a vibrant spectrum of natural flavors and nourishing benefits, inviting a transformative approach to wellness and vitality. Picture this: a kaleidoscope of fruits and vegetables at your fingertips, each one holding the promise of improved health, energy, and a deeper connection to the natural world. Juicing is not just a culinary activity; it's a celebration of life's pure essences, distilled into every glass.

At its core, juicing is the process of extracting the liquid treasure from fruits and vegetables, leaving behind the pulp and fiber. This liquid gold is packed with vitamins, minerals, and phytonutrients, offering a direct infusion of health into your system. Unlike eating whole fruits and vegetables, juicing delivers these nutrients in a more digestible form, allowing your body to absorb them more readily. It's like giving your digestive system a luxurious vacation, where all it has to do is bask in the nutritional abundance without the extra work of breaking down solid food.

For those new to this green and vibrant world, the idea of juicing might seem daunting or shrouded in mystery. Yet, the essence of juicing is rooted in simplicity and an ancestral connection to the earth. Our forebears understood the value of consuming plants for health, and juicing is a modern extension of this ancient wisdom. It's a bridge to a more holistic way of living, where we're not just eating to satiate hunger, but nourishing our bodies at the deepest level.

Imagine starting your day not with the jarring buzz of an alarm, but with the serene ritual of crafting a juice. The act itself is meditative, a moment of calm in the whirlwind of daily life. You select your ingredients with care, wash them gently, and then watch as they transform, combining their strengths into something greater than the sum of their parts. This isn't merely food preparation; it's a daily ritual of self-care and respect for the bounty of nature.

Juicing introduces you to a world of flavors you might never have encountered otherwise. The sweetness of a ripe apple, the zesty punch of ginger, the earthy tones of beetroot, and the refreshing crispness of cucumber can all play starring roles in your juice creations. Each ingredient not only brings its unique taste but also its unique health benefits, contributing to a holistic approach to wellness.

Beyond the health benefits, juicing fosters a deeper connection to your food. In a world where meals are often consumed on the go, juicing invites you to slow down, to become more mindful of what you're putting into your body. It's an opportunity to reflect on the journey of each fruit and vegetable, from the soil to your table, reminding us of our place in the larger web of life.

Yet, juicing is not a one-size-fits-all solution. It's a journey of discovery, where each individual can find their own path to wellness. Some may embrace juicing as a daily practice, while others might see it as a vibrant addition to their existing diet. The beauty of juicing lies in its flexibility, in the ability to tailor it to your own lifestyle, needs, and tastes.

As we delve into the world of juicing, we'll explore not just the "how" but the "why." It's not enough to know which button to press on your juicer; understanding the profound impact that juicing can have on your health and well-being is what transforms this from a mere trend into a sustainable lifestyle choice. Juicing is an invitation to engage more deeply with the world around you, to listen to your body's needs, and to nourish yourself with the pure essence of life. In embracing juicing, you're not just adding a new habit to your routine; you're opening the door to a world of enhanced wellness, vitality, and connection. It's a journey that begins with a single sip but leads to a profound transformation in how you view food, health, and life itself. Welcome to the wondrous world of juicing, where every glass is a step toward a healthier, more vibrant you.

# Understanding the Basics

Diving into the world of juicing is akin to opening a door to a garden of vibrant possibilities, where each fruit and vegetable holds the potential for transformative health benefits. To walk this path with confidence, it's crucial to grasp the fundamentals that form the bedrock of juicing. This understanding not only enriches your juicing experience but also ensures you're extracting the maximum nutritional value from your chosen produce.

At its heart, juicing is the art and science of separating the juice from the fiber of fruits and vegetables, concentrating the liquid essence brimming with vitamins, minerals, and phytonutrients into a drinkable form. This process makes the nutrients more readily available to your body, as it doesn't have to work through the fiber to access them. It's a direct line to nourishment, offering a unique way to consume the bounty of the plant kingdom.

The journey begins with choosing the right equipment. The juicer, your companion on this voyage, comes in various shapes and sizes, each suited to different preferences and lifestyles. Centrifugal juicers, for instance, are the speedsters of the juicing world, using a fast-spinning blade to extract juice. They're ideal for the busy individual looking for quick results. On the other hand, masticating juicers, often referred to as slow juicers, use a gear to crush the produce at a deliberate pace, yielding more juice and preserving the nutritional integrity of the ingredients. Understanding the strengths and limitations of each type of juicer will guide you in selecting the one that aligns with your goals and routines.

Selecting your produce is the next foundational step. The cornucopia of fruits and vegetables available offers a palette of flavors and health benefits. However, not all produce is created equal. Learning to choose high-quality, ripe, and, when possible, organic ingredients can significantly enhance the nutritional value and taste of your juice. This choice not only impacts your health but also supports sustainable agriculture practices.

The basics of juicing also encompass a knowledge of how to combine ingredients effectively. The symphony of flavors available through juicing is vast, but understanding the notes is key to creating harmonious blends. For example, leafy greens serve as a nutrient-dense base, while fruits can add natural sweetness, and ingredients like ginger or lemon inject a zing that elevates the overall experience. Balancing these elements is an art, one that enriches your body and delights your palate.

Juicing, however, is more than just a method of nutrient extraction; it's a commitment to a lifestyle that prioritizes health and wellness. Integrating juicing into your daily routine requires a shift in mindset, recognizing it not as a mere diet addition but as a step towards holistic well-being. This shift is where the basics of juicing intertwine with the rhythms of daily life, making juicing a sustainable practice rather than a fleeting endeavor.

Moreover, understanding the basics involves recognizing the importance of cleaning and maintenance. A juicer is not just a tool but a partner in your health journey. Proper care ensures its longevity and efficiency, making your juicing routine smoother and more enjoyable. This aspect might seem mundane, but it's fundamental to a hassle-free juicing experience.

In addition to equipment and ingredient basics, there's the aspect of nutritional understanding. Juicing offers a concentrated source of nutrients, but it's essential to be mindful of the balance in your overall diet. For instance, while juicing can significantly increase your intake of vitamins and minerals, it's also crucial to consume whole fruits and vegetables to ensure you're getting enough fiber. This balanced approach ensures that you're not only benefiting from the immediate impact of juicing but also supporting your long-term health and digestive well-being. As you embark on this juicing journey, remember that the basics are not just steps to be followed but pillars on which to build your personal health philosophy. Each glass of juice is a reflection of your commitment to nurturing your body, a tangible manifestation of wellness that starts from within. Understanding the basics of juicing is the first sip in a lifelong journey of health and vitality, a journey that promises not just a spectrum of flavors but a transformation of your well-being.

## Setting Up Your Juicing Space

Creating a dedicated juicing space in your home is akin to establishing a personal wellness sanctuary—a place where health goals are not just imagined but actively pursued and achieved. This space becomes the heart of your juicing journey, a physical manifestation of your commitment to nourishing your body and spirit. It's where the magic happens, where raw fruits and vegetables are transformed into liquid gold, brimming with vitality and life.

The first step in setting up your juicing space is choosing the right location. It should be a place that invites you in, making the process of juicing feel not like a chore but a cherished ritual. Whether it's a sunny corner of your kitchen or a spacious countertop, the key is accessibility and comfort. You want everything you need at arm's reach, allowing the process to flow as smoothly as the juices you'll create.

Your juicer, the cornerstone of this space, should be chosen with care, reflecting your needs and the frequency of your juicing. Positioning it as the focal point of your juicing area not only makes it easier to use but also serves as a constant reminder of your health commitments. Surrounding your juicer, you'll need ample space for preparation—cutting boards, knives, and bowls for sorting your produce. This setup is not just about functionality; it's about creating a space that feels good to be in, one that inspires and motivates you.

Lighting plays a crucial role in this setup. Natural light can enhance the vibrancy of the fruits and vegetables, making the act of juicing a more visually appealing and uplifting experience. If natural light isn't abundant, consider bright, warm artificial lighting that mimics the sun's glow, ensuring your juicing space is inviting at any time of day.

Storage is another critical element of your juicing space. Having a dedicated spot for your juicing essentials—reusable produce bags, glass storage bottles for your juice, and any supplements or powders you incorporate—can streamline your process. This might include shelving or cabinets close to your juicing station, designed to keep everything organized and within reach. The goal is to minimize clutter, which not only makes juicing more enjoyable but also reinforces a sense of calm and order in your wellness practice.

The aesthetics of your juicing space can significantly impact your motivation and enjoyment of the process. Consider incorporating elements that resonate with your personal style and wellness philosophy. This could be as simple as a vase of fresh flowers, inspirational quotes on the wall, or a color scheme that soothes and energizes you. Your juicing space should be a reflection of your journey towards health and wellness, personalized to make it uniquely yours.

Hygiene and maintenance are also paramount. Your juicing space should be easy to clean, with non-porous surfaces and storage solutions that keep your tools and workspace hygienic. Investing in quality cleaning tools and making a habit of cleaning after each juicing session can keep the space inviting and ready for use. This practice not only ensures your juicing space is physically clean but also contributes to a mental state of clarity and preparedness for your wellness routines.

Finally, consider the ergonomics of your juicing space. The height of your countertop, the ease of accessing your juicer and ingredients, and the comfort of standing or sitting while juicing can all affect how frequently you engage with the process. Your juicing station should be a place where you can comfortably spend time, reflecting on your health goals and enjoying the process of working towards them.

In crafting your juicing space, you're doing more than just setting up an area for preparing juice; you're creating a sanctuary for wellness, a corner of your home dedicated to nurturing your body and soul. This space is a tangible commitment to your health journey, designed to support and inspire you every step of the way. It's where each day's promise of vitality and well-being begins, with the simple act of juicing transforming into a profound ritual of self-care and nourishment.

## Tips for Juicing Success

Embarking on a juicing journey is much like setting sail on uncharted waters. It holds the promise of discovery, the potential for transformation, and the excitement of new horizons. Yet, the true essence of navigating this voyage lies not just in the destination but in understanding the nuances of the journey itself. Success in juicing is a mosaic made up of various pieces—knowledge, preparation, and the cultivation of a mindset geared towards wellness.

The foundation of juicing success begins with a commitment to learning. Understanding the nutritional profile of your ingredients is crucial. Each fruit and vegetable you choose is a character in the story you're telling, with its own set of benefits and flavors. But it's the synergy among these characters that creates a narrative rich in health and vitality. It's about more than just taste; it's about crafting a potion that nurtures your body, caters to your needs, and aligns with your health goals.

Preparation, both mental and physical, is your compass in this journey. It involves planning your recipes, sourcing quality produce, and organizing your juicing space for efficiency and inspiration. But it also means preparing your mind for the changes ahead. Juicing is a habit, a ritual that becomes woven into the fabric of your daily life. Embrace it not as a chore but as an act of self-care, an investment in your health that deserves time and attention.

The art of juicing is also about embracing variety. The natural world is abundant with fruits, vegetables, and herbs, each offering its unique palette of flavors and nutrients. Diversifying your ingredients not only prevents boredom but also ensures your body receives a wide range of vitamins, minerals, and antioxidants. It's akin to painting with a broad spectrum of colors, each stroke adding depth and vibrancy to your wellness canvas.

Yet, even the most colorful journey has its challenges. One of the most common hurdles is managing waste. The pulp left behind, though often overlooked, is rich in fiber and nutrients. Instead of seeing it as waste, view it as an opportunity. Use it to make compost for your garden, add it to baked goods for extra fiber, or incorporate it into broths and soups. This approach not only maximizes your investment in produce but also aligns with a sustainable lifestyle, respecting the bounty nature provides.

Success in juicing also hinges on consistency. Like any journey of transformation, the benefits of juicing unfold over time. It requires patience, persistence, and a commitment to making juicing a regular part of your routine. It's about finding joy in the process, celebrating the small victories, and recognizing that each glass of juice is a step closer to your wellness goals.

Moreover, juicing is a personal journey. What works for one may not work for another. It's important to listen to your body and adjust your juicing practices accordingly. Some may thrive on green juices, while others may prefer the sweetness of fruits. Some may juice daily, while others may find a few times a week sufficient. The key is to find your rhythm, one that harmonizes with your lifestyle and your body's needs.

In this journey, remember that education is ongoing. The world of health and wellness is ever-evolving, with new research, techniques, and ingredients continually emerging. Stay curious, open to learning, and willing to experiment. It's this spirit of exploration that keeps the journey exciting and ensures your juicing practices remain aligned with the latest in nutritional science.

Lastly, share your journey. Juicing, at its core, is an act of love—love for oneself and for the vibrant world of fruits and vegetables. Sharing your creations, your learnings, and your successes can inspire others to embark on their own journeys. It creates a community of wellness, a collective celebration of health and vitality.

Juicing is not just a culinary activity; it's a pathway to wellness, a practice that nourishes the body, calms the mind, and soothes the soul. With each glass of juice, you're not just ingesting nutrients; you're absorbing life force, the very essence of nature's bounty. By embracing these tips for juicing success, you set sail on a voyage of discovery, one that promises not just health and vitality but a deeper connection to the world around you.

# 2. Unveiling the Health Advantages of Juicing

## Nutritional Benefits of Juicing

When we talk about juicing, we're diving into a world where nature's bounty meets human ingenuity to create a symphony of health benefits, with each sip delivering a concentrated dose of nature's best. The act of juicing strips away the solid fibers of fruits and vegetables, leaving us with the essence of their nutrients—a liquid elixir that can revitalize, restore, and rejuvenate our bodies from the inside out.

At the heart of juicing's allure is its direct line to nutritional wealth. Fruits and vegetables are storehouses of vitamins, minerals, enzymes, and phytonutrients, elements foundational to our health and wellbeing. Juicing makes these nutrients more accessible, especially to those who struggle to meet their daily recommended intake of fruits and vegetables. It's a bridge over the gap between knowing what's good for us and actually getting those nutrients into our body.

Imagine the process of juicing as a form of pre-digestion. Your juicer breaks down these foods in a way that your digestive system would, but it does so without the fiber. This means that the vitamins and minerals contained in your juice can be absorbed into your bloodstream more quickly, providing almost immediate benefits to your health. It's akin to giving your body a direct infusion of energy and nourishment—without the heavy lifting required to digest whole fruits and vegetables.

This accessibility of nutrients is particularly beneficial when considering the modern diet, which often falls short of the variety and quantity of fruits and vegetables recommended for optimal health. Juicing allows for a creative and enjoyable way to increase your intake of these essential food groups, making it easier to reach nutritional goals that might otherwise seem daunting. But juicing's benefits extend beyond merely hitting daily vitamin and mineral targets. The phytonutrients found in plants—compounds like flavonoids, carotenoids, and polyphenols—play significant roles in protecting our bodies from disease. They have antioxidant properties, fighting against the oxidative stress that contributes to aging and chronic diseases. By incorporating a wide range of fruits and vegetables into your juices, you're not just consuming nutrients; you're arming your body with a diverse arsenal of compounds that can bolster your health in myriad ways.

Moreover, the process of juicing can also lead to the consumption of a broader variety of fruits and vegetables than one might typically include in their diet. Many of us are creatures of habit, often eating the same foods day after day. Juicing opens up a world of variety, encouraging experimentation with different flavors and ingredients. This not only makes for a more interesting dietary experience but also diversifies the range of nutrients you consume, further enhancing your overall nutritional profile.

Another crucial aspect of juicing's nutritional benefits is its impact on alkalinity in the body. A diet high in processed foods, meats, and dairy can lead to a more acidic internal environment, which has been linked to various health issues. Fruits and vegetables, on the other hand, are inherently alkaline-forming. Consuming them in juice form can help balance your body's pH, contributing to improved bone health, reduced inflammation, and a lower risk of chronic diseases.

It's also worth noting the role of juicing in hydration. While not a replacement for water, the high liquid content of juice—especially when made from water-rich fruits and vegetables like cucumbers, celery, and melons—can contribute to your daily fluid intake. Proper hydration is essential for every function of the body, from maintaining energy levels to ensuring healthy skin.

In embracing juicing, it's important to proceed with awareness and balance. While juicing delivers concentrated nutrients, it should complement, not replace, whole fruits and vegetables in your diet. Fiber, found in the pulp and skins of produce, is essential for digestive health and helps regulate blood sugar levels. Including a mix of whole foods and juices ensures you're getting the full spectrum of health benefits that fruits and vegetables have to offer.

In conclusion, the nutritional benefits of juicing are both broad and profound. From providing a concentrated source of vitamins and minerals to encouraging a diverse and alkaline-rich diet, juicing can be a powerful tool in your wellness arsenal. It's a testament to the idea that sometimes, the simplest methods—turning whole fruits and vegetables into liquid gold—can be the most transformative for our health.

## Enhancing Digestive Health

Embarking on a journey to enhance digestive health through juicing is akin to rediscovering the natural rhythms and needs of your body. It's a process that honors the body's intricate system, providing it with the essential tools to rejuvenate, repair, and function with renewed vigor. The act of juicing can be a key ally in this journey, offering a spectrum of benefits that support and nurture the digestive system, the cornerstone of our overall health and wellbeing.

Digestive health is the linchpin of our body's ability to absorb nutrients, eliminate toxins, and maintain a balanced internal ecosystem. In the modern diet, rich in processed foods and lacking in whole fruits and vegetables, the digestive system often bears the brunt of poor dietary choices. Juicing offers a pathway back to wellness, delivering nutrient-rich liquids that are not only easy on the digestion but also packed with the enzymes, vitamins, and minerals needed to support and enhance digestive function.

At the heart of juicing's benefits for digestive health is the concept of "pre-digestion." The process of juicing breaks down the cell walls of fruits and vegetables, essentially doing much of the digestive system's work. This means that the body can absorb the nutrients more efficiently, without the added burden of breaking down fiber. For individuals with sensitive digestion or conditions like IBS, juicing can provide a much-needed reprieve, allowing the digestive system to rest and recover while still receiving ample nutrition.

Moreover, the high enzyme content in fresh juices plays a pivotal role in digestive health. Enzymes are the catalysts for every biological process in the body, including digestion. Many fruits and vegetables are rich in natural enzymes that can help break down food more effectively, enhancing nutrient absorption and optimizing digestive function. Pineapple, for example, contains bromelain, while papaya has papain—both are proteolytic enzymes that aid in the digestion of proteins.

The alkalizing effect of many juices is another boon for digestive health. An overly acidic environment in the stomach and intestines can lead to discomfort, inflammation, and a host of digestive issues. Juices made from green vegetables and certain fruits can help balance the body's pH, creating a more favorable environment for digestion and nutrient absorption. This not only supports the digestive process but also promotes a healthy gut microbiome, the community of beneficial bacteria that plays a crucial role in our health.

Hydration is another critical aspect of digestive health that juicing addresses. Proper hydration is essential for digestion, as it helps break down food, absorb nutrients, and move waste through the intestines. Juicing, especially when it includes cucumber, celery, and other water-rich vegetables, can significantly contribute to daily fluid intake, supporting healthy digestion and preventing issues like constipation and bloating.

Incorporating a variety of juices into your diet can also introduce a wider range of prebiotics—fibers that feed beneficial gut bacteria. While juicing removes most of the fiber, the remnants that remain in the juice can still offer some prebiotic benefits. Additionally, the act of juicing encourages the consumption of a broader array of fruits and vegetables, many of which contain unique fibers and compounds that support a healthy gut microbiome.

It's important to approach juicing as part of a balanced diet that also includes whole fruits and vegetables, to ensure that you're getting enough dietary fiber. Fiber is essential for digestive health, promoting regular bowel movements and acting as a food source for beneficial gut bacteria. A holistic approach to juicing, one that sees it as a complement rather than a replacement for whole foods, is key to reaping its digestive health benefits.

In crafting a juicing regimen that supports digestive health, consider starting with vegetables and fruits known for their digestive benefits, such as ginger for its soothing properties, mint for easing indigestion, and fennel for reducing bloating. Experimenting with these ingredients can help you discover combinations that not only taste good but also support your digestive system. Embracing juicing as a pathway to enhancing digestive health is an invitation to connect more deeply with the needs of your body. It's a practice that requires mindfulness, experimentation, and a commitment to nurturing your health from the inside out. By providing your body with nutrient-rich juices, you're not just nourishing your cells; you're supporting a foundational aspect of your health, setting the stage for greater vitality and wellbeing.

# Boosting Immunity and Energy

In the quest for enhanced well-being, juicing emerges as a beacon of vitality, illuminating a path to bolstered immunity and invigorated energy. This liquid alchemy, transforming fruits and vegetables into nutrient-dense elixirs, offers more than mere hydration. It's a profound communion with nature's apothecary, each sip a step closer to optimal health.

The essence of juicing's power lies in its concentrated delivery of vitamins, minerals, and antioxidants. These nutrients are the vanguards of our immune system, fortifying our body's defenses against pathogens. Vitamin C, a luminary in immune support, abounds in citrus fruits, kale, and bell peppers. Its antioxidant prowess helps neutralize free radicals, reducing inflammation and boosting immune resilience. Juicing provides a palatable avenue to consume these ingredients in quantities that might be challenging to eat whole, ensuring your body receives a potent dose of this essential nutrient.

Equally vital to immune health is vitamin A, with its stellar role in maintaining the integrity of mucosal barriers, including those in the gut and lungs, which serve as first lines of defense against infection. Carrots, spinach, and sweet potatoes, transformed into vibrant juices, become a delicious source of this key vitamin, enhancing the body's barrier against pathogens.

The synergy of nutrients in fresh juices extends beyond vitamins to include trace minerals like zinc and selenium, lesser celebrated but no less crucial for immune function. Zinc, found in spinach, and selenium, present in certain fruits, contribute to the proper functioning of immune cells, fortifying the body's response to invaders. Juicing, by combining these elements, creates a holistic defense strategy, weaving a tapestry of nutrients that work in concert to protect and energize the body.

Beyond bolstering immunity, juicing is a veritable fountain of energy. The natural sugars in fruits provide a quick, clean source of fuel, while the absence of fiber ensures rapid absorption, offering an instant uplift in vitality. This energy boost is not the fleeting surge delivered by processed sugars but a sustained lift that nourishes cells and supports metabolic processes. Moreover, the enzymes present in raw juices play a pivotal role in energy production. Acting as catalysts in biochemical reactions, these enzymes facilitate the efficient conversion of food into energy, enhancing cellular function and vitality. In a culture where fatigue is often combated with caffeine and stimulants, juicing offers a restorative alternative, energizing the body through nutrition rather than temporary fixes.

Juicing's impact on energy and immunity is also mediated through detoxification. The liver, a linchpin in the body's detoxifying machinery, benefits from the compounds in green juices, such as chlorophyll, which can aid in the neutralization and removal of toxins. A cleaner internal environment allows the immune system to function more efficiently and improves overall energy levels, as the body is not bogged down by the task of processing toxins.

The hydrating effect of juices further supports detoxification and energy. Proper hydration is crucial for all bodily functions, including immune response and energy production. Juices, particularly those made from cucumbers, celery, and watermelon, offer a delicious way to meet hydration needs, ensuring that the body's systems operate smoothly and energetically.

Adopting a juicing regimen also invites an exploration of a diverse array of fruits and vegetables, each with its unique profile of phytonutrients. These compounds, while not essential for basic survival, confer significant health benefits, including immune modulation and energy enhancement. For instance, the flavonoids in berries and the carotenoids in carrots have been shown to support immune health through their anti-inflammatory and antioxidant properties.

In navigating the journey to bolstered immunity and energy through juicing, it's essential to embrace variety, balance, and moderation. A juice cleanse or an all-juice diet is not the panacea for health; rather, juicing should complement a diet rich in whole foods, providing a spectrum of fiber, nutrients, and benefits. It's also critical to listen to the body's cues, adjusting juice ingredients and quantities to suit individual health needs and goals.

Juicing, in essence, is an act of kindness towards the body, a nurturing gesture that conveys respect for its complex needs. It's a commitment to nourishing oneself with the pure, life-affirming essence of fruits and vegetables. In this act lies the potential for transformative health benefits, including a robust immune system and a reservoir of energy to navigate life's demands with resilience and vitality.

## Detoxification and Weight Management

In the landscape of health and wellness, juicing stands out as a beacon of light for those navigating the often murky waters of detoxification and weight management. This method of consuming nature's bounty offers a straightforward yet profound way to support the body's natural cleansing processes while also aiding in the management of weight. The essence of juicing—transforming fresh, whole fruits and vegetables into liquid form—provides a nutrient-dense solution that can complement the body's efforts to purify and balance itself.

Detoxification is the body's ongoing process of neutralizing and eliminating toxins from tissues and organs. A well-designed juicing regimen can enhance this natural detoxification by supplying the body with an abundance of vitamins, minerals, and phytonutrients. These components act synergistically to support liver function, the cornerstone of the detox process, and other vital systems involved in cleansing the body. The liver, with its complex and multifaceted role in filtering blood, breaking down toxins, and metabolizing nutrients, benefits greatly from the influx of compounds such as glutathione and antioxidants found in leafy greens and cruciferous vegetables. By juicing these plant foods, we deliver these powerful substances in concentrations that are sometimes more difficult to achieve through whole foods alone.

Moreover, the hydration provided by juice concoctions plays a crucial role in the detoxification process. Adequate fluid intake is essential for maintaining healthy kidney function, allowing the body to excrete toxins through urine. Juices made from cucumbers, celery, and water-rich fruits not only contribute to hydration but also supply a range of electrolytes and phytonutrients that support the body's natural cleansing processes.

When it comes to weight management, juicing offers a unique advantage by providing a low-calorie, nutrient-rich beverage option. For individuals looking to reduce their caloric intake without sacrificing nutritional quality, juicing can be a powerful tool. The key lies in selecting the right ingredients. Vegetables, particularly leafy greens, should form the base of juices for weight management, as they are low in calories yet high in fiber, vitamins, and minerals. Fruits, while also nutritious, are higher in natural sugars and should be used judiciously to sweeten juices without adding excessive calories.

Juicing can also play a role in appetite control and satiety. While it's true that juice lacks the fiber found in whole fruits and vegetables, which is essential for satiety and digestive health, the liquid form of these nutrients can still help curb hunger pangs by providing a satisfying taste experience. Incorporating juicing into a balanced diet, where whole foods provide the necessary fiber, allows for the enjoyment of juices as a complement to meals or as a healthy snack alternative. It's important to approach juicing for weight management as part of a holistic lifestyle strategy. This means integrating juicing with a balanced diet rich in whole foods, regular physical activity, and adequate hydration. Juice cleanses or extreme juice fasting are not sustainable long-term strategies for weight loss and can potentially lead to nutrient deficiencies and other health issues. Instead, juicing should be viewed as one component of a diverse and balanced dietary approach.

In crafting juices for detoxification and weight management, diversity is key. A wide variety of fruits and vegetables ensures a broad spectrum of nutrients. Ingredients such as ginger and lemon not only add flavor but also possess properties that support metabolism and detoxification. Herbs like parsley and cilantro can offer additional detoxifying benefits, making them excellent additions to any juice blend aimed at cleansing and weight management. In conclusion, juicing provides a versatile and effective tool for enhancing the body's natural detoxification processes and assisting in weight management. By carefully selecting ingredients and incorporating juicing into a balanced lifestyle, individuals can enjoy the myriad benefits that these nutrient-dense beverages have to offer. Whether seeking to support the body's cleansing efforts or to manage weight healthily, juicing offers a pathway to achieving these goals, grounded in the power of whole-food nutrition and the body's innate wisdom.

# 3. Preparing Your Produce: Best Practices

## Selecting Quality Fruits and Vegetables

In the journey of juicing, the first step is pivotal: selecting quality fruits and vegetables. This initial choice lays the groundwork for the nutritional value, taste, and overall success of your juicing endeavors. Think of it as building a foundation for a house; the stronger and more robust the materials, the more solid and enduring the structure.

When it comes to choosing produce for juicing, understanding what constitutes 'quality' is key. Quality is not merely about the external appeal of fruits and vegetables, though a vibrant appearance can be indicative of freshness. It's about seeking out produce that offers the highest nutritional content, the best flavor, and the least amount of contaminants like pesticides and herbicides.

The search for quality begins with seasonality. Seasonal fruits and vegetables are not only fresher but they have also traveled shorter distances to reach your table, making them more environmentally friendly options. They are typically harvested at their peak of ripeness, ensuring maximum flavor and nutritional value. Engaging with local farmers markets or subscribing to a community-supported agriculture (CSA) box are excellent ways to access seasonal produce and also to learn more about where and how your food is grown.

Organoleptic qualities—those involving taste, sight, smell, and touch—provide immediate clues to the freshness and quality of produce. Look for fruits and vegetables that are firm to the touch, free from blemishes or soft spots, and vibrant in color. The aroma should be fresh and reminiscent of the earth; a strong, sweet smell may indicate overripeness, while a lack of scent might suggest under-ripeness.

Understanding the source of your produce is also crucial. Organic fruits and vegetables, grown without synthetic pesticides, fertilizers, or genetically modified organisms (GMOs), are often recommended for juicing. They tend to have lower pesticide residues and may have higher nutritional value. While organic produce can be more expensive, the investment in health is generally considered worthwhile. If budget constraints make buying entirely organic difficult, familiarize yourself with the Environmental Working Group's (EWG) "Dirty Dozen" and "Clean Fifteen" lists, which identify the fruits and vegetables with the highest and lowest pesticide residues.

The integrity of the produce is paramount. Fruits and vegetables that have been mechanically damaged or bruised can lose nutritional value more rapidly than their intact counterparts. Such damage may also make produce more susceptible to bacteria and mold, which can compromise both safety and taste. Careful handling and selection can mitigate these risks.

In addition to selecting high-quality produce, consider the diversity of your choices. A wide range of fruits and vegetables not only enhances the flavor profile of your juices but also ensures a broad spectrum of vitamins, minerals, and antioxidants. Each color in produce represents a different set of phytonutrients, so incorporating a rainbow of colors in your juicing regimen maximizes health benefits. For those seeking the pinnacle of quality and nutritional value, heirloom varieties of fruits and vegetables offer a unique proposition. These traditional varieties, passed down through generations, are often grown in smaller batches and can offer superior taste and nutrient profiles compared to their mass-produced counterparts. While not always readily available in conventional grocery stores, they can often be found at farmers markets or specialty food shops.

Finally, building relationships with local farmers and produce vendors can provide invaluable insights into selecting the best fruits and vegetables for juicing. These experts can offer advice on peak seasonality, how to spot the freshest produce, and even tips on rare or particularly nutritious varieties. In crafting juices that nourish the body, invigorate the spirit, and delight the palate, the art of selecting quality produce cannot be overstated. It's a practice that requires patience, knowledge, and a bit of intuition. But the rewards—a vibrant spectrum of flavors, a wealth of health benefits, and the satisfaction of connecting more deeply with the food we consume—are immeasurable. Selecting quality fruits and vegetables is not just a step in the process of juicing; it's a commitment to excellence and well-being.

## Cleaning and Prepping Techniques

Embarking on a juicing journey transforms the kitchen into a sanctuary of health, where each fruit and vegetable is a building block for nourishment and vitality. Before these ingredients can be transformed into vibrant, nutrient-packed juices, they must undergo a crucial phase of preparation. This process is not merely a routine but a ritual that enhances the quality of your juice, ensuring that every drop is as pure and beneficial as nature intended.

The cornerstone of this ritual is thorough cleaning. Given the concerns about pesticides, bacteria, and other contaminants, washing your produce is paramount. However, it's not just about running fruits and vegetables under cold water. The goal is to remove as much residue and as many microbes as possible without compromising the integrity of the produce.

For starters, consider soaking your fruits and vegetables in a solution of water and vinegar, a natural disinfectant, for a few minutes. This method has been shown to reduce surface contaminants more effectively than water alone. A ratio of 1 part vinegar to 3 parts water is typically recommended. For items with tougher skins or more noticeable residue, using a produce brush during this soak can help dislodge particles that cling to the surface.

After soaking, rinsing your produce under running water is a critical next step. This washes away any lingering vinegar taste along with the loosened contaminants. For leafy greens, a salad spinner can be invaluable, helping to remove water and ensuring that your greens are dry and ready for juicing. When it comes to prepping your produce, the approach varies by type. Root vegetables like carrots and beets should be scrubbed to remove any dirt and then trimmed to remove parts that could harbor more bacteria or contaminants. Leafy greens, on the other hand, should be inspected leaf by leaf, removing any wilted or discolored parts before washing.

Fruits come with their own set of preparation rules. Citrus fruits, for example, are best juiced when peeled to avoid the bitter taste of the rind, but leave the white pith as it's packed with nutrients. Apples and pears can be juiced with their skins on for additional fiber and vitamins, but remember to remove the seeds and core. Berries, with their delicate nature, should be gently washed and used whole. The importance of cutting and chopping your produce cannot be understated. This step is not just about making fruits and vegetables fit into your juicer. It's about increasing the surface area exposed to the juicer's mechanism, which can enhance juice yield and preserve the nutritional content. However, it's crucial to size these pieces appropriately to not overwhelm your juicer, ensuring a smooth and efficient juicing process. For those concerned with maintaining the utmost nutritional integrity, consider the timing of your prep work. Cutting fruits and vegetables can expose their inner nutrients to air and light, leading to oxidation. This natural process can diminish some of the produce's nutritional value over time. To mitigate this, prepare your produce close to the time of juicing. If you must prep in advance, storing your cut fruits and vegetables in airtight containers in the refrigerator can help preserve their freshness and nutritional content. Beyond these practical steps, the act of preparing your produce for juicing is an opportunity to connect with the food you consume. It's a moment to appreciate the colors, textures, and scents of fruits and vegetables, grounding yourself in the experience of creating healthful, life-affirming juices. This mindfulness, combined with meticulous preparation techniques, elevates the simple act of juicing into a nourishing practice for both body and soul. In embracing these cleaning and prepping techniques, you're not just ensuring the purity and safety of your juices. You're honoring the natural goodness of your ingredients, crafting juices that are not only a delight to the palate but a profound source of health and energy. It's a testament to the idea that the best results come from not only what we do but how we do it—with care, with attention, and with respect for the natural world that sustains us.

# The Importance of Organic Produce

In the realm of juicing, the quality of the ingredients directly influences the quality of the juice. This truth brings the conversation to the forefront about the significance of choosing organic produce. Opting for organic is not merely a lifestyle choice; it's a commitment to health, environmental sustainability, and supporting agricultural practices that respect the earth and its inhabitants.

Organic produce is cultivated without the use of synthetic pesticides, herbicides, and fertilizers. These substances, commonplace in conventional farming, are designed to kill or repel pests and enhance growth but can have unintended consequences for the produce, the environment, and human health. Residues from these chemicals can remain on (and in) fruits and vegetables, potentially making their way into your juice. By choosing organic, you minimize your exposure to these compounds, aligning your juicing practice with a broader intention of consuming clean, unadulterated foods.

But the benefits of organic produce extend beyond the absence of synthetic chemicals. Organic farming practices are designed to work in harmony with nature, promoting soil health, biodiversity, and ecological balance. Healthy soil produces healthy plants, which in turn offer higher nutritional value. Studies have indicated that organic fruits and vegetables can contain higher levels of certain nutrients, including antioxidants, compared to their conventionally grown counterparts. When you juice with organic produce, you're tapping into this enhanced nutritional profile, ensuring that every sip delivers a potent dose of health-promoting compounds.

The importance of organic produce also lies in its impact on the planet. Organic farming methods reduce pollution and conserve water, contributing to a healthier and more sustainable environment. The avoidance of synthetic chemicals means healthier soil and waterways, benefiting not just the current but future generations. By supporting organic agriculture through your choice of produce for juicing, you're casting a vote for a type of farming that prioritizes the planet's well-being over convenience and short-term yield.

Moreover, choosing organic supports ethical farming practices that prioritize the health and welfare of farmworkers. Traditional farming methods that rely heavily on chemical pesticides and fertilizers can expose workers to harmful substances, posing risks to their health and safety. Organic farming minimizes these risks, creating safer working conditions and fostering communities that value and respect their labor force.

In embracing organic produce for juicing, it's also vital to recognize the challenges, including availability and cost. Not everyone has easy access to a wide variety of organic fruits and vegetables, and when available, they can be more expensive than conventional produce. However, investing in organic, when possible, is an investment in health, environmental stewardship, and ethical consumption. For those navigating these barriers, focusing on the "Dirty Dozen" and "Clean Fifteen" lists can help prioritize organic purchases where they're most impactful. In conclusion, the choice to use organic produce in juicing is a multifaceted decision that touches on health, environmental sustainability, and ethical considerations. It's about more than just the absence of pesticides—it's about participating in a food system that values quality, ecology, and human dignity. As you prepare your produce for juicing, choosing organic where possible is a profound step toward nurturing not just your own health, but the health of the planet and its people.

## Storing Your Ingredients for Freshness

The art of juicing begins long before fruits and vegetables are transformed into vibrant, nutrient packed elixirs. It starts with the careful selection of ingredients and extends through the meticulous process of cleaning and preparation. Yet, one of the most critical steps in ensuring the quality and nutritional integrity of your juice is often overlooked: the proper storage of your ingredients.

Maintaining the freshness of fruits and vegetables is pivotal not just for flavor but for preserving their vital nutrients and enzymes. The journey to optimal storage begins with understanding the unique needs of each type of produce. Not all fruits and vegetables thrive under the same conditions; some require the cool, dark confines of a refrigerator, while others are best kept at room temperature.

For leafy greens, which are staples in many juice recipes for their health benefits, moisture is both friend and foe. These vegetables need a humid environment to stay crisp but can quickly wilt or rot if they become too damp. Storing them in the refrigerator in a produce bag with a paper towel can help manage moisture levels, keeping them fresh and ready for juicing. Similarly, herbs, often used to add a burst of flavor and nutrients to juices, benefit from being stored in water, like a bouquet of flowers, with their stems trimmed and covered loosely with a plastic bag in the fridge.

Root vegetables, on the other hand, prefer a cool, dark place. A basement or a root cellar is ideal, but a dark corner of a pantry can also suffice. If refrigerated, they should be placed in the crisper drawer to minimize moisture loss, ensuring they remain firm and juicy until they're ready to be juiced.

Citrus fruits and apples present a unique storage dilemma. While they can be kept at room temperature for a short period, refrigeration extends their shelf life and preserves their juicy, tangy qualities essential for adding a zing to any juice. However, they should be stored separately; fruits like apples emit ethylene gas, which can accelerate ripening and spoilage in other produce.

Berries, a favorite for adding sweetness and color to juices, are delicate and prone to mold. They should be refrigerated and kept dry in their original container, with any spoiled berries removed to prevent the spread of mold. Washing berries just before juicing, rather than before storage, helps maintain their integrity and prevents premature spoilage.

Tomatoes, avocados, and bananas, which some adventurous juicers incorporate for texture and nutrition, are best stored on the countertop, where they can ripen to perfection. Once ripe, avocados and bananas can be moved to the refrigerator to slow down the ripening process, while tomatoes are best kept at room temperature to preserve their flavor and texture.

Understanding the ethylene factor is crucial for all produce storage. Ethylene-producing fruits like bananas, avocados, and tomatoes should be kept away from ethylene-sensitive produce like leafy greens and berries to prevent premature ripening and spoilage.

Lastly, investing in quality storage solutions, such as produce-specific containers or bags that regulate airflow and humidity, can make a significant difference in extending the freshness of fruits and vegetables. Regularly rotating your stock and keeping an eye on expiration dates ensures that only the freshest, most vibrant ingredients make their way into your juicer.

In the world of juicing, where every ingredient counts, the careful storage of fruits and vegetables is not just a practice in prolonging shelf life. It's a commitment to flavor, nutrition, and the sanctity of each juice you create. By giving your ingredients the care they deserve, you honor the journey from farm to table to juicer, ensuring that each sip is a testament to the beauty and bounty of the natural world.

# 4. Diversifying Your Juicing Experience

## Exploring Additives and Superfoods

Embarking on a juicing journey opens a canvas of culinary creativity, inviting an exploration that goes beyond the simplicity of fruits and vegetables. The inclusion of additives and superfoods into your juicing regimen is not just about enhancing flavors—it's an opportunity to infuse your creations with an extra layer of nutrition and health benefits. This exploration into the world of additives and superfoods transforms each glass of juice from a mere beverage into a potent elixir of health. Superfoods—a term that has captured the imagination of health enthusiasts and nutritionists alike—refer to foods that are exceptionally high in vitamins, minerals, antioxidants, enzymes, and other health-promoting compounds. When we talk about integrating these powerhouses into juices, we're looking at amplifying the nutritional profile of each sip. Imagine a drink that not only refreshes but also delivers a concentrated burst of immune-boosting, energy-enhancing, and disease-fighting properties. One of the most celebrated superfoods is spirulina, a blue-green algae that packs a hefty punch of protein, vitamins B1, B2, and B3, iron, and magnesium. A small spoonful of spirulina powder can turn your morning juice into a protein-rich drink that supports muscle strength and endurance, making it a favorite among athletes and fitness enthusiasts.

Chia seeds, another superfood, offer a different set of benefits. Rich in omega-3 fatty acids, fiber, and calcium, these tiny seeds can be soaked in water to form a gel-like substance that blends seamlessly into juices, adding a satisfying texture while promoting heart health and digestion.

The realm of additives also includes a variety of powders, seeds, and extracts, each bringing its unique blend of benefits. Maca powder, derived from the root of the maca plant, is renowned for its ability to enhance energy and stamina without the jitters associated with caffeine. Its malty, nutty flavor adds a subtle richness to juices, making them not only more nutritious but also more palatable.

For those looking to support their immune system, camu camu powder is an excellent additive. This Amazonian fruit is one of the richest sources of vitamin C on the planet, far outstripping the more common oranges and strawberries. A sprinkle of camu camu can elevate a simple juice into a powerful antioxidant drink that combats free radicals and supports overall health.

The list of potential additives is vast and varied, including everything from bee pollen, known for its allergy-fighting properties, to turmeric, celebrated for its anti-inflammatory and antioxidant effects. The key is to experiment with these ingredients, finding combinations that not only taste good but also align with your health goals and nutritional needs.

Integrating additives and superfoods into your juicing is also an exercise in balance. The goal is not to overload your juices but to enhance them. It's about finding the right mix that complements the natural flavors of your fruits and vegetables while boosting the nutritional value of your creations. Start with small amounts, gradually increasing as you become familiar with the flavors and effects of each additive.

In embracing the world of additives and superfoods, you're not just diversifying your juicing experience; you're taking a proactive step towards a more nutritious lifestyle. Each juice becomes a custom-crafted potion, tailored to your specific health requirements and taste preferences. It's an adventurous foray into the potential of natural foods, an exploration that makes juicing not just a part of your diet, but a vibrant part of your health and wellness journey.

This exploration into additives and superfoods reflects a broader understanding of juicing as not merely a dietary habit but a holistic health practice. It's an invitation to experiment, learn, and grow in your health journey, leveraging the power of nature's most potent foods to enhance your well-being, one juice at a time.

# Balancing Flavors

In the vibrant world of juicing, the mastery of balancing flavors is akin to an art form, where each ingredient plays a pivotal role in creating a harmonious blend. This balance is not just about making a juice palatable; it's about enhancing the nutritional experience, ensuring each sip is a symphony of taste that nurtures both body and soul. Achieving this equilibrium requires an understanding of the flavor profiles of fruits and vegetables, and how they interact when combined. It's a journey of exploration, experimentation, and, ultimately, personalization.

At the heart of flavor balancing is the concept of the flavor wheel, which encompasses the five basic tastes: sweet, sour, salty, bitter, and umami. Sweetness, often provided by fruits like apples, oranges, and pineapples, is the backbone of many juices, appealing to our innate preference for sugar. However, when left unchecked, sweetness can overpower a juice, masking the other flavors. Herein lies the role of sourness, offered by citrus fruits like lemons and limes, which can cut through the sweetness, adding a refreshing sharpness that elevates the juice.

Bitterness, though often shunned, has its place in the juicing palette. Leafy greens such as kale, dandelion, and arugula introduce a bitter edge that can add depth and complexity to juices, while also boosting their nutritional content. The key is to balance bitterness with the other tastes, ensuring it complements rather than overwhelms. Salty flavors, though less common in juicing, can be subtly introduced through ingredients like celery or a pinch of sea salt, enhancing the overall flavor profile and bringing out the natural sweetness and freshness of the fruits and vegetables.

Umami, the savory taste, is less prevalent in fruit and vegetable juices but can be incorporated through the addition of tomatoes, which provide a richness and complexity that rounds out the juice, making it more satisfying and full-bodied.

Achieving balance also involves considering the mouthfeel and body of the juice, which can be influenced by the ingredients' texture and water content. Creamier fruits like bananas and avocados can add thickness and smoothness, making the juice more substantial, while watery cucumbers and melons can lighten it up, making it more refreshing.

The color of the juice, too, plays a subtle yet important role in the perception of taste. Vibrant colors can make a juice more appealing and enticing, suggesting freshness and vitality. By carefully selecting and combining ingredients, one can create visually stunning juices that are as delightful to the eyes as they are to the palate.

Personal tastes and preferences ultimately guide the process of balancing flavors. What constitutes the perfect balance for one person may differ for another, making it essential to experiment and adjust according to individual likes and dislikes. Starting with small batches and making minor adjustments in ingredient ratios can help in fine-tuning the flavors to one's preference.

In the end, balancing flavors in juicing is about creating a beverage that is not only nutritious but also enjoyable to drink. It's about transforming simple fruits and vegetables into a beverage that delights the senses, enriches the body, and satisfies the soul. Through the thoughtful combination of ingredients, mindful of their flavors, textures, and nutritional benefits, one can craft juices that are truly a joy to consume, making the juicing experience both rewarding and delicious.

## Creative Combinations

Diving into the world of juicing with the intent to diversify your experience is akin to embarking on a culinary adventure, where the blending of flavors and ingredients knows no bounds. The art of creating creative combinations in juicing not only enhances the sensory enjoyment of your drink but also maximizes the nutritional benefits, making each glass a bespoke concoction tailored to your health goals and taste preferences.

The canvas for creativity in juicing is vast, with an almost infinite array of fruits, vegetables, herbs, and superfoods at your disposal. The key to unlocking this potential lies in stepping beyond conventional pairings and embracing the unexpected. It's about marrying the sweet with the savory, the earthy with the tangy, and discovering in the process that the whole is indeed greater than the sum of its parts.

Consider, for example, the unconventional but harmonious pairing of beetroot and berries. Beets, with their deep, earthy flavor and rich nutritional profile, offer a grounding base. Berries, on the other hand, bring a bright pop of sweetness and a high antioxidant count. Together, they create a juice that's not only visually stunning, with its vibrant red hue, but also a powerhouse of nutrients that support heart health and fight inflammation.

Venturing into the realm of savory juices opens up another dimension of creative combinations. Incorporating vegetables like kale, spinach, and celery with a touch of green apple and lemon can yield a juice that's refreshingly green and bursting with vitamins and minerals essential for detoxification and energy. The addition of a slice of ginger or a sprinkle of cayenne pepper can introduce a warm, spicy undertone that elevates the juice from merely nutritious to invigoratingly flavorful.

The exploration of creative combinations also invites the use of ingredients that may not traditionally be associated with juicing. Avocado, for instance, can add a creamy texture and a dose of healthy fats, making your juice more satiating. Cucumber and mint, when combined, create a drink that's not only hydrating but also remarkably refreshing, perfect for cooling down on a hot day or after a vigorous workout.

Another avenue for creativity lies in thematic juicing, where you craft your blends around a specific health goal or nutritional theme. A "Sunrise Juice" might feature orange, carrot, and a touch of turmeric, each ingredient chosen for its ability to boost immunity and provide a vibrant start to the day. A "Detox Green Juice" could blend several types of leafy greens with apple, lemon, and parsley, focusing on ingredients known for their cleansing properties.

The process of discovering creative combinations is also a journey of learning and experimentation. It involves understanding the flavor profile and nutritional benefits of each ingredient and considering how they might complement or contrast with one another. It's about tasting, adjusting, and sometimes starting over, with each iteration bringing you closer to your ideal blend. Ultimately, the pursuit of creative combinations in juicing is an expression of personal taste and nutritional needs. It's a way to keep your juicing routine exciting and varied, ensuring that you're not only nourishing your body with essential vitamins and minerals but also delighting your palate with each sip. In this creative exploration, the possibilities are endless, limited only by your imagination and willingness to experiment. So, go ahead, mix and match, blend and taste, and discover the joy of creating your own unique juice combinations.

## Experimenting with Herbs and Spices

Embarking on a journey to diversify your juicing experience by experimenting with herbs and spices is akin to unlocking a treasure chest of flavors and health benefits. This exploration is not merely about adding complexity to the taste of your juices; it's a profound engagement with ancient traditions and modern nutrition, where each herb and spice plays a pivotal role in enhancing both the sensory and medicinal qualities of your concoctions.

Herbs and spices have been revered through the ages for their healing properties and their ability to elevate food and drink into something sublime. Incorporating these potent botanicals into your juices introduces a new dimension of wellness and flavor. It's a dance of the delicate and the robust, the sweet and the savory, creating a harmony that invigorates the palate and nourishes the body.

Imagine the zest of ginger root added to a carrot and apple juice, transforming a simple beverage into a warming, digestive aid that soothes the stomach and fires up the metabolism. Or consider the refreshing coolness of mint in a watermelon and cucumber juice, offering not just a burst of freshness but also acting as a natural stimulant that can improve mental alertness and relieve digestive discomfort.

Turmeric, with its vibrant golden hue, is another marvel of the spice world, known for its anti-inflammatory properties and ability to support immune function. A pinch of turmeric in a juice blend of orange, pineapple, and coconut water can yield a potent anti-inflammatory drink, rich in antioxidants and delightfully tropical in taste.

Cilantro, often polarizing due to its unique flavor, is a powerhouse of detoxification benefits, binding to heavy metals and facilitating their elimination from the body. When juiced with pineapple, green apple, and lime, it creates a detoxifying elixir that's as beneficial for the liver as it is refreshing.

The use of spices need not be overt; a subtle hint can be transformative. A dash of cinnamon in a pear and spinach juice can regulate blood sugar levels, while a sprinkle of cayenne pepper in a tomato and red bell pepper juice can boost circulation and increase nutrient absorption.

Experimenting with herbs and spices in juicing also invites a deeper understanding of their individual properties and how they can be combined for specific health outcomes. It's an opportunity to tailor your juicing practice to your personal health needs, whether it's boosting immunity, enhancing digestion, or calming inflammation.

Moreover, this exploration is an exercise in creativity and personal taste. It's about finding the right balance where the flavors of the herbs and spices complement rather than overpower the fruits and vegetables. It encourages a playful approach to juicing, where trial and error lead to discovery and delight.

In essence, experimenting with herbs and spices in juicing is about more than just diversifying your beverage repertoire; it's a holistic practice that bridges the gap between nutrition and pleasure, between ancient wisdom and contemporary wellness. It's an invitation to explore the vast world of flavors and health benefits that these botanicals offer, making each glass of juice a celebration of life's vibrant diversity.

This exploration into the use of herbs and spices in juicing reflects a broader commitment to a lifestyle that values natural, healthful, and flavorful nourishment. It's a testament to the power of nature's bounty and the endless possibilities that await when we open ourselves to the art and science of juicing.

# 5. Crafting Fruit-Centric Juices

## Sweet and Tangy Recipes

### Recipe 1: Mango Tango Citrus Blast

**P.T.:** 10 minutes

**Ingr.:**

2 ripe mangoes, peeled and cubed

1 orange, peeled and segmented

1 lime, juiced

1/2 lemon, juiced

1 tablespoon of honey (optional, for added sweetness)

A pinch of salt to enhance flavor

Ice cubes (optional, for serving)

**Servings:** 2

**M.C.:** Blending

**Procedure:**

In a blender, combine the mango cubes, orange segments, lime juice, and lemon juice.

Add honey and a pinch of salt.

Blend until smooth. If the mixture is too thick, you can add a small amount of water to reach your desired consistency. Taste and adjust the sweetness with more honey if desired.

Serve over ice cubes in tall glasses for a refreshing drink.

**N.V.:** Rich in Vitamin C and A.

### Recipe 2: Strawberry Lemonade Zing

**P.T.:** 5 minutes

**Ingr.:**

Fresh strawberries

lemon juice

water

agave syrup

ice

**Servings:** 2

**M.C.:** Blending

**Procedure:**

Blend strawberries with lemon juice, water, and agave until smooth.

Serve chilled.

**N.V.:** High in Vitamin C, low in calories.

### Recipe 3: Pineapple Ginger Spark

**P.T.:** 7 minutes

**Ingr.:**

Pineapple

ginger root

lime juice

water

honey

**Servings:** 2

**M.C.:** Blending and straining

**Procedure:**

Combine pineapple, ginger, lime juice, and water; blend and strain.

Sweeten with honey.

**N.V.:** Boosts digestion, rich in vitamins.

## Recipe 4: Blueberry Pomegranate Bliss

**P.T.:** 10 minutes

**Ingr.:**

Blueberries,

 pomegranate seeds,

apple juice,

mint leaves.

**Servings:** 2

**M.C.:** Blending

**Procedure:**

Blend all ingredients until smooth, garnish with mint.

**N.V.:** Antioxidant-rich, good for heart health.

## Recipe 5: Kiwi Cucumber Cooler

**P.T.:** 8 minutes

**Ingr.:**

Kiwi

cucumber

mint

lemon juice

sparkling water.

**Servings:** 2

**M.C.:** Mixing

**Procedure:**

Mix kiwi and cucumber juice with lemon; top with sparkling water.

**N.V.:** Hydrating, rich in Vitamin K.

## Recipe 6: Raspberry Lime Rickey

**P.T.:** 5 minutes

**Ingr.:**

Raspberries

lime juice

sparkling water

ice

honey

**Servings:** 2

**M.C.:** Blending

**Procedure:**

Blend raspberries with lime and honey, mix in sparkling water.

**N.V.:** Fiber-rich, low in calories.

## Recipe 7: Citrus Burst Sunshine

**P.T.:** 6 minutes

**Ingr.:**

Orange

grapefruit

carrots

lemon juice

turmeric

**Servings:** 2

**M.C.:** Juicing

**Procedure:**

Juice all ingredients, serve with a dash of turmeric.

**N.V.:** Boosts immunity, anti-inflammatory.

### Recipe 8: Watermelon Lemonade

**P.T.:** 4 minutes

**Ingr.:**

Watermelon

lime juice

mint leaves

ice

water

**Servings:** 2

**M.C.:** Blending

**Procedure:**

Blend watermelon with lime juice and water, serve over ice.

**N.V.:** Hydrating, rich in lycopene.

### Recipe 9: Peachy Keen Ginger Squeeze

**P.T.:** 7 minutes

**Ingr.:**

Peaches

ginger root

lemon juice

water

honey

**Servings:** 2

**M.C.:** Blending

**Procedure:**

Blend peaches with ginger and lemon, sweeten with honey.

**N.V.:** Good for digestion, Vitamin A.

### Recipe 10: Tart Cherry Elixir

**P.T.:** 5 minutes

**Ingr.:**

Tart cherries

apple juice

lemon juice

water

**Servings:** 2

**M.C.:** Blending

**Procedure:**

Blend cherries with apple and lemon juice, dilute with water as needed.

**N.V.:** Supports sleep, rich in antioxidants.

# Seasonal Fruit Juices

## Recipe 1: Green Goddess Revival

**P.T.:** 5 minutes

**Ingr.:**

2 cups of kale destemmed and chopped

1 cup of spinach, fresh

1/2 cucumber, chopped

1 green apple, cored and sliced

1/2 lemon, juiced

1 inch piece of ginger, peeled

1/2 cup of water or coconut water for blending

**Servings:** 2

**M.C.:** Blending

**Procedure:**

Place the kale, spinach, cucumber, and green apple into a high-speed blender.

Add the lemon juice and ginger.

Pour in the water or coconut water to help the blending process.

Blend on high until the mixture is smooth and fully combined.

If desired, strain the juice for a smoother texture or enjoy it as is for extra fiber.

**N.V.:** Rich in Vitamin A, Vitamin C, and iron from the leafy greens.

## Recipe 2: Autumn Apple Spice

**P.T.:** 5 minutes

**Ingr.:**

2 apples

1/4 tsp ground cinnamon

a pinch of nutmeg

1 inch fresh ginger

**Servings:** 2

**M.C.:** Juicing

**Procedure:**

Juice the apples and ginger, then stir in the cinnamon and nutmeg.

Serve immediately for a warm spice kick.

**N.V.:** High in dietary fiber (if pulp included), Vitamin C, and antioxidants.

## Recipe 3: Tropical Winter Boost

**P.T.:** 7 minutes

**Ingr.:**

1 cup pineapple chunks

1 mango

peeled and pitted

juice of 1 orange

juice of 1/2 lime

**Servings:** 2

**M.C.:** Blending

**Procedure:**

Blend all ingredients until smooth, adding a splash of water if needed.

Strain for a smoother texture.

**N.V.:** Rich in Vitamin C, Vitamin A, and enzymes aiding digestion.

## Recipe 4: Spring Melody

**P.T.:** 5 minutes

**Ingr.:**

2 kiwis

1 cup strawberries

handful of mint leaves

**Servings:** 2

**M.C.:** Blending

**Procedure:**

Blend kiwis, strawberries, and mint with a bit of water until smooth.

Serve fresh.

**N.V.:** High in Vitamin C, dietary fiber, and antioxidants.

## Recipe 5: Early Summer Peach Splash

**P.T.:** 5 minutes

**Ingr.:**

2 peaches

1 nectarine

a dash of vanilla extract

**Servings:** 2

**M.C.:** Blending

**Procedure:**

Blend peaches, nectarine, and vanilla with ice until smooth.

Enjoy this sweet, creamy delight.

**N.V.:** Good source of Vitamins A and C, and antioxidants.

## Recipe 6: Late Summer Watermelon Wave

**P.T.:** 5 minutes

**Ingr.:**

4 cups cubed watermelon

juice of 1 lime

handful of mint leaves

**Servings:** 2

**M.C.:** Blending

**Procedure:**

Puree watermelon, lime juice, and mint until smooth. Chill and serve.

**N.V.:** Hydrating, rich in lycopene and Vitamin C.

## Recipe 7: Fall Pomegranate Passion

**P.T.:** 8 minutes

**Ingr.:**

Seeds from 1 pomegranate

1 pear

a sprinkle of cinnamon.

**Servings:** 2

**M.C.:** Blending

**Procedure:**

Juice pomegranate and pear, mix with cinnamon.

Serve immediately to enjoy a burst of fall flavors.

**N.V.:** Loaded with antioxidants, fiber, and Vitamin C.

## Recipe 8: Winter Citrus Blast

**P.T.:** 5 minutes

**Ingr.:**

2 oranges

1 grapefruit

2 carrots

**Servings:** 2

**M.C.:** Juicing

**Procedure:**

Juice all ingredients and serve chilled for a refreshing and immune-boosting drink.

**N.V.:** High in Vitamin C, beta-carotene, and flavonoids.

## Recipe 9: Spring Green Reviver

**P.T.:** 6 minutes

**Ingr.:**

1 green apple

2 stalks celery

1 cup spinach

1/2 lemon, juiced

**Servings:** 2

**M.C.:** Juicing

**Procedure:**

Juice all ingredients, stirring in the lemon juice at the end.

Enjoy this detoxifying green juice.

**N.V.:** Rich in chlorophyll, vitamins, and minerals, aiding in detoxification and digestion.

## Recipe 10: Sunny Citrus Cooler

**P.T.:** 5 minutes

**Ingr.:**

Juice of 2 lemons

juice of 2 limes

juice of 2 oranges

sparkling water

**Servings:** 4

**M.C.:** Mixing

**Procedure:**

Mix all the citrus juices in a pitcher, then fill with sparkling water for a fizzy, refreshing drink.

**N.V.:** An excellent source of Vitamin C, hydration, and a refreshing alternative to sugary sodas.

# Citrus Blends

### Recipe 1: Sunrise Citrus Symphony

**P.T.:** 5 minutes

**Ingr.:**

2 oranges, peeled

1 grapefruit, peeled and deseeded

1 lemon, peeled and deseeded

1 lime, peeled and deseeded

1 teaspoon of honey (optional)

A pinch of salt

**Servings:** 2

**M.C.:** Blending

**Procedure:**

Combine oranges, grapefruit, lemon, and lime in a blender.

Add honey and a pinch of salt to enhance the flavors.

Blend until smooth. For a thinner consistency, add a little water.

Strain the blend to remove any excess pulp, if desired.

Serve chilled for a refreshing start to your day.

**N.V.:** Rich in Vitamin C, promoting immune health.

### Recipe 2: Citrus Zest Cooler

**P.T.:** 5 minutes

**Ingr.:**

1 orange, peeled and segmented

1 lime juiced

1 lemon juiced

2 cups sparkling water

A handful of fresh mint leaves, for garnish

**Servings:** 2

**M.C.:** Mixing

**Procedure:**

In a large pitcher, combine the orange segments, lime juice, and lemon juice.

Add sparkling water and stir gently to mix.

Garnish with fresh mint leaves.

Serve chilled for a refreshing drink.

**N.V.:** Low in calories, rich in Vitamin C, and provides hydration.

## Recipe 3: Tropical Citrus Blast

**P.T.:** 7 minutes

**Ingr.:**

1/2 grapefruit peeled and segmented

1 orange peeled and segmented

Juice of 1 lime

1/2 cup pineapple chunks

1 cup coconut water

**Servings:** 2

**M.C.:** Blending

**Procedure:**

Place grapefruit, orange, lime juice, and pineapple chunks in a blender.

Add coconut water for a tropical flavor and hydration.

Blend until smooth and well combined.

Serve immediately for a refreshing tropical citrus experience.

**N.V.:** High in Vitamin C, potassium, and antioxidants.

## Recipe 4: Lemon Lime Fusion

**P.T.:** 5 minutes

**Ingr.:**

2 lemons juiced

2 limes juiced

1-inch piece of ginger, peeled and minced

2 tablespoons honey (adjust to taste)

Ice cubes, for serving

**Servings:** 2

**M.C.:** Blending

**Procedure:**

Juice the lemons and limes, and place the juice in a blender.

the minced ginger and honey to the blender.

Blend until the ginger is finely mixed with the juices.

Pour over ice cubes in glasses and serve for a zesty, refreshing drink.

**N.V.:** Good source of Vitamin C, aids digestion, and has anti-inflammatory properties.

## Recipe 5: Citrus Ginger Spark

**P.T.:** 6 minutes

**Ingr.:**

1 orange juiced

1 lemon juiced

1 lime, juiced

1-inch piece of ginger grated

1/4 teaspoon turmeric powder

1 tablespoon honey (optional)

**Servings:** 2

**M.C.:** Mixing

**Procedure:**

In a pitcher, combine the juices of orange, lemon, and lime.

Add grated ginger and turmeric powder to the mix.

Stir in honey to sweeten if desired.

Mix well and serve over ice for an energizing drink.

**N.V.:** Packed with anti-inflammatory properties, boosts immunity, and aids in digestion.

## Recipe 6: Sweet Citrus Surprise

**P.T.:** 5 minutes

**Ingr.:**

2 blood oranges, juiced

1 tangerine, juiced

1 carrot, juiced

1-inch piece of ginger juiced

1 tablespoon honey (optional)

**Servings:** 2

**M.C.:** Juicing

**Procedure:**

Juice the blood oranges, tangerine, carrot, and ginger using a juicer.

Combine all the juices in a pitcher.

Stir in honey if a sweeter taste is desired.

Serve chilled to enjoy a nutrient-packed, sweet citrus drink.

**N.V.:** Rich in vitamins A and C, aids in immune function and digestion.

## Recipe 7: Citrus Mint Refresh

**P.T.:** 5 minutes

**Ingr.:**

Juice of 2 limes

Juice of 1 lemon

Juice of 1 orange

1 liter of sparkling water

Fresh mint leaves, for garnish

Ice cubes, for serving

**Servings:** 4

**M.C.:** Mixing

**Procedure:**

In a large pitcher, mix together the lime, lemon, and orange juice.

Add sparkling water and stir gently to combine.

Add ice cubes to glasses and pour the citrus mixture over.

Garnish each glass with fresh mint leaves.

Serve immediately for a refreshing and uplifting beverage.

**N.V.:**

A low-calorie drink that's high in vitamin C and antioxidants. Mint adds a refreshing twist and aids digestion.

## Recipe 8: Spicy Citrus Wake-Up

**P.T.:** 5 minutes

**Ingr.:**

Juice of 1 grapefruit

Juice of 2 oranges

Juice of 1 lemon

A pinch of cayenne pepper

1 tablespoon of maple syrup (or to taste)

**Servings:** 2

**M.C.:** Mixing

**Procedure:**

Combine grapefruit, orange, and lemon juice in a mixing bowl.

Add a pinch of cayenne pepper and maple syrup to the juice mixture. Stir well.

Taste and adjust the sweetness or spiciness as desired.

Serve the juice in glasses over ice for a spicy kick start to your day.

**N.V.:**

Rich in vitamins A and C, metabolism-boosting cayenne, and natural sweetness from maple syrup.

## Recipe 9: Citrus Beet Elixir

**P.T.:** 8 minutes

**Ingr.:**

Juice of 2 oranges

Juice of 1 grapefruit

Juice of 1 lemon

1 small beet, peeled and juiced

1 tablespoon honey (optional)

**Servings:** 2

**M.C.:** Juicing

**Procedure:**

Use a juicer to obtain juice from the oranges, grapefruit, lemon, and beet.

Combine all the juices in a pitcher and stir well.

Sweeten with honey if desired and stir until fully dissolved.

Serve chilled for a nutrient-dense, energizing drink.

**N.V.:**

Offers detoxifying benefits, high in folate from beets, and packed with vitamin C.

## Recipe 10: Green Citrus Twist

**P.T.:** 7 minutes

**Ingr.:**

Juice of 2 limes

Juice of 1 lemon

1 green apple, cored and sliced

1 cup spinach leaves

1/2 cucumber, sliced

**Servings:** 2

**M.C.:** Blending

**Procedure:**

In a blender, combine lime and lemon juice, green apple slices, spinach leaves, and cucumber.

Blend until the mixture is smooth. For a thinner consistency, add a little water.

Taste and adjust the flavor as needed, adding more lime or lemon juice for extra zing.

Serve immediately for a refreshing and health-boosting green juice.

**N.V.:** High in dietary fiber, vitamin C, and antioxidants. The green apple and cucumber provide a hydrating base, while spinach adds iron and other minerals.

## Exotic Fruit Combinations

### Recipe 1: Dragonfruit Delight

**P.T.:** 10 minutes

**Ingr.:**

1 dragonfruit, peeled and cubed

1 cup of pineapple chunks

Juice of 1 lime

1 teaspoon of honey (optional)

1/2 cup of coconut water

**Servings:** 2

**M.C.:** Blending

**Procedure:**

Place dragonfruit, pineapple chunks, and lime juice into a blender.

Add honey for a touch of sweetness if desired.

Pour in coconut water for a smooth consistency.

Blend until smooth.

Serve chilled for a refreshing and hydrating exotic juice.

**N.V.:** High in Vitamin C, antioxidants, and hydration properties.

### Recipe 2: Passionate Mango Tango

**P.T.:** 8 minutes

**Ingr.:**

2 ripe mangoes, peeled and cubed

Pulp of 2 passion fruits

Juice of 1 orange

1/2 cup of papaya, cubed

Mint leaves for garnish

**Servings:** 2

**M.C.:** Blending

**Procedure:**

Combine mangoes, passion fruit pulp, orange juice, and papaya in a blender.

Blend until the mixture is smooth and creamy.

Garnish with mint leaves for a refreshing aroma.

Serve immediately to enjoy a burst of tropical flavors.

**N.V.:** Rich in Vitamins A and C, fiber, and antioxidants.

## Recipe 3: Kiwi Quencher

**P.T.:** 5 minutes

**Ingr.:**

4 kiwis, peeled and sliced

1 cup green grapes

1/2 honeydew melon, cubed

Ice cubes (optional)

**Servings:** 2

**M.C.:** Blending

**Procedure:**

Combine kiwis, green grapes, and honeydew melon in a blender.

Add ice cubes for a chilled beverage.

Blend until smooth.

Serve immediately for a refreshing and nutrient-packed drink.

**N.V.:** Rich in Vitamin C, Vitamin K, and dietary fiber, with energizing natural sugars.

## Recipe 4: Tropical Berry Bliss

**P.T.:** 10 minutes

**Ingr.:**

1/2 cup acai berries (fresh or frozen)

1 cup strawberries, hulled

1/2 cup coconut milk

Juice of 1 lime

**Servings:** 2

**M.C.:** Blending

**Procedure:**

Place acai berries, strawberries, coconut milk, and lime juice in a blender.

Blend until creamy and smooth.

Serve chilled, garnished with a few whole strawberries for a burst of antioxidants in a creamy, dreamy smoothie.

**N.V.:** High in antioxidants, healthy fats from coconut milk, and Vitamin C.

## Recipe 5: Guava Glow

**P.T.:** 7 minutes

**Ingr.:**

3 guavas, seeded and cut into chunks

2 carrots, peeled and chopped

1-inch piece of ginger, peeled

**Servings:** 2

**M.C.:** Juicing

**Procedure:**

Pass guavas, carrots, and ginger through a juicer.

Stir the juice well to combine the flavors.

Serve the juice immediately, or chilled, to enjoy a vibrant, immune-boosting drink.

**N.V.:** Loaded with Vitamin C, beta-carotene, and anti-inflammatory properties.

## Recipe 6: Lychee Lush

**P.T.:** 5 minutes

**Ingr.:**

1 cup lychees, peeled and pitted

2 peaches, sliced

1 teaspoon rose water

**Servings:** 2

**M.C.:** Blending

**Procedure:**

In a blender, combine lychees, peaches, and rose water.

Blend until smooth.

Serve chilled for a fragrant and refreshing drink.

**N.V.:** Offers Vitamin C, dietary fiber, and antioxidants with a unique floral aroma.

## Recipe 7: Pomegranate Persuasion

**P.T.:** 8 minutes

**Ingr.:**

Seeds from 2 pomegranates

1 cup cherries, pitted

1 cup cranberries (fresh or if using dried, ensure they're unsweetened and soak them in water for a few hours)

**Servings:** 2

**M.C.:** Blending and straining

**Procedure:**

Combine pomegranate seeds, cherries, and cranberries in a blender.

Blend until fully mashed up.

Strain through a fine mesh to remove the pulp.

Serve the juice chilled for a deeply nourishing and antioxidant-rich beverage.

**N.V.:** High in antioxidants, Vitamin C, and manganese, great for heart health and reducing inflammation.

## Recipe 8: Soursop Serenity

**P.T.:** 10 minutes

**Ingr.:**

1 cup soursop (graviola), peeled and seeded

1 cup pineapple chunks

Juice of 1 lime

A handful of mint leaves

**Servings:** 2

**M.C.:** Blending

**Procedure:**

Blend soursop, pineapple, lime juice, and mint leaves until smooth.

Serve immediately for a tropical, cancer-fighting concoction.

**N.V.:** Rich in antioxidants, vitamins, and minerals. Known for its anti-cancer properties and ability to boost the immune system.

## Recipe 9: Carambola Citrus Splash

**P.T.:** 5 minutes

**Ingr.:**

2 starfruits (carambola), sliced

Juice of 2 oranges

1/2 cup sparkling water

**Servings:** 2

**M.C.:** Blending

**Procedure:**

Blend starfruits and orange juice until smooth.

Stir in sparkling water for a fizzy effect.

Serve chilled for a refreshing and hydrating drink.

**N.V.:** High in Vitamin C, antioxidants, and hydrating properties.

# 6. Delving into Vegetable Juices

## Leafy Greens and Their Benefits

### Recipe 1: Kale and Spinach Elixir

**P.T.:** 5 minutes

**Ingr.:**

2 cups kale, destemmed and chopped

2 cups spinach, fresh

1 apple, cored and sliced

1/2 cucumber, sliced

Juice of 1 lemon

1 inch piece of ginger, peeled

1/2 cup of water

**Servings:** 2

**M.C.:** Blending

**Procedure:**

Add kale, spinach, apple, cucumber, lemon juice, and ginger to a high-powered blender.

Pour in water to facilitate blending.

Blend on high until the mixture is smooth.

If desired, strain the juice through a fine mesh strainer for a smoother texture.

Serve immediately to enjoy a nutrient-packed juice.

**N.V.:** High in vitamins A, C, and K, iron, calcium, and antioxidants. The ginger adds digestive benefits, while lemon boosts the vitamin C content and aids in iron absorption.

### Recipe 2: Celery Cilantro Cleanse

**P.T.:** 5 minutes

**Ingr.:**

4 celery stalks, chopped

1 cup cilantro, leaves and stems

1 green apple, cored and sliced

Juice of 1 lime

1/4 jalapeño, seeded (optional for a spicy kick)

1/2 cup water

**Servings:** 2

**M.C.:** Blending

**Procedure:**

Place celery, cilantro, green apple, lime juice, and jalapeño (if using) into a blender.

Add water to help blend smoothly.

Blend until completely smooth.

Strain through a fine mesh sieve for a smoother texture, if desired.

Serve chilled for a refreshing detox drink.

**N.V.:** Rich in vitamins A, C, and K, antioxidants, and aids in detoxification and digestion.

## Recipe 3: Minty Pea Shoot Drink

**P.T.:** 7 minutes

**Ingr.:**

1 cup pea shoots

1/2 cup mint leaves

1 green apple, cored and sliced

Juice of 1 lime

1/2 cup water

**Servings:** 2

**M.C.:** Blending

**Procedure:**

Combine pea shoots, mint leaves, green apple, and lime juice in a blender.

Add water to facilitate blending.

Blend until the mixture is smooth.

Serve immediately for a unique, nutrient-packed green juice.

**N.V.:** High in vitamin C, dietary fiber, and antioxidants. Pea shoots also provide a good amount of plant-based protein.

## Recipe 4: Swiss Chard Citrus Boost

**P.T.:** 6 minutes

**Ingr.:**

2 cups Swiss chard leaves, chopped

1 orange, peeled and segmented

1 carrot, chopped

1 inch piece of ginger, peeled

1/2 cup water or orange juice

**Servings:** 2

**M.C.:** Juicing/Blending

**Procedure:**

If using a juicer, pass Swiss chard, orange, carrot, and ginger through the juicer.

For blending, combine all ingredients in a blender with water or orange juice for a smoother consistency.

Serve immediately to enjoy a vibrant, energizing drink.

**N.V.:** Excellent source of vitamins A, C, and K, plus the ginger provides anti-inflammatory benefits.

## Recipe 5: Collard Green Pineapple Zest

**P.T.:** 8 minutes

**Ingr.:**

2 cups collard greens, stems removed and chopped

1 cup pineapple chunks

1 cucumber, chopped

A handful of mint leaves

1/2 cup water

**Servings:** 2

**M.C.:** Blending

**Procedure:**

Add collard greens, pineapple, cucumber, and mint leaves to a blender.

Pour in water to help blend the ingredients smoothly.

Blend until completely smooth.

Serve chilled for a refreshing, tropical-flavored green juice.

**N.V.:** Loaded with vitamins C and A, calcium, and powerful antioxidants.

## Recipe 6: Arugula Apple Tango

**P.T.:** 5 minutes

**Ingr.:**

2 cups arugula

1 large green apple, cored and sliced

Juice of 1 lemon

1 stalk of celery, chopped

1/2 cup water

**Servings:** 2

**M.C.:** Blending

**Procedure:**

Combine arugula, green apple, lemon juice, celery, and water in a blender.

Blend until smooth.

Serve immediately, offering a peppery yet sweet juice that's sure to awaken your taste buds.

**N.V.:** Rich in vitamin C, potassium, and antioxidants. Arugula is also a good source of calcium.

## Recipe 7: Mustard Greens Melody

**P.T.:** 7 minutes

**Ingr.:**

2 cups mustard greens, chopped

1 pear, cored and sliced

1/2 fennel bulb, chopped

Juice of 1/2 lemon

1/2 cup water

**Servings:** 2

**M.C.:** Blending

**Procedure:**

Place mustard greens, pear, fennel, and lemon juice into a blender.

Add water for desired consistency.

Blend until smooth for a slightly spicy, sweet, and refreshing juice.

**N.V.:** High in fiber, vitamin C, and unique compounds that may support detoxification processes.

## Recipe 8: Beet Greens and Berry

**P.T.:** 10 minutes

**Ingr.:**

2 cups beet greens, chopped

1 cup mixed berries (strawberries, blueberries, raspberries)

1 small beet, peeled and chopped

1 banana

1/2 cup almond milk or water

**Servings:** 2

**M.C.:** Blending

**Procedure:**

Add all ingredients to a blender, starting with the liquid to ensure smooth blending.

Blend until the mixture is creamy and smooth.

Serve immediately for a sweet, nutrient-dense smoothie packed with antioxidants.

**N.V.:** Provides a good source of dietary fiber, vitamins A, C, and K, as well as potassium and magnesium.

### Recipe 9: Dandelion Detox Delight

**P.T.:** 5 minutes

**Ingr.:**

2 cups dandelion greens, washed

1 apple, cored and sliced

1 cucumber, sliced

Juice of 1 lemon

1 inch piece of ginger, peeled

1/2 cup water

**Servings:** 2

**M.C.:** Blending

**Procedure:**

Combine dandelion greens, apple, cucumber, lemon juice, ginger, and water in a blender. Blend until smooth for a powerful detoxifying and liver-supportive green juice.

**N.V.:** High in vitamins A, C, E, and K, iron, calcium, and detoxifying compounds.

### Recipe 10: Watercress Wellness Wave

**P.T.:** 6 minutes

**Ingr.:**

2 cups watercress

1 cup pineapple chunks

1 mango, peeled and cubed

1/2 cup coconut water

**Servings:** 2

**M.C.:** Blending

**Procedure:**

Add watercress, pineapple, mango, and coconut water to a blender.

Blend until smooth for a hydrating and immune-boosting juice.

**N.V.:** Rich in antioxidants, vitamin C, and compounds that may have cancer-preventive properties.

# Root Vegetable Recipes

## Recipe 1: Carrot Ginger Glow

**P.T.:** 5 minutes

**Ingr.:**

4 large carrots, peeled and chopped

1-inch piece of ginger, peeled

Juice of 1 orange

1 teaspoon turmeric powder

1/2 cup water (optional for blending)

**Servings:** 2

**M.C.:** Juicing or blending

**Procedure:**

If using a juicer, pass carrots and ginger through the juicer. Stir in orange juice and turmeric powder.

For blending, combine all ingredients in a blender, add water as needed, and blend until smooth. Strain through a nut milk bag or fine sieve.

Serve chilled for a refreshing and invigorating juice.

**N.V.:** High in vitamin A from carrots, vitamin C from orange, and anti-inflammatory properties from turmeric and ginger.

## Recipe 2: Beetroot and Apple Bliss

**P.T.:** 10 minutes

**Ingr.:**

2 medium beetroots, peeled and chopped

2 apples, cored and chopped

1/2 lemon, peeled

1-inch piece of ginger, peeled

1/2 cup water or apple juice (optional for blending)

**Servings:** 2

M.C.: Juicing or blending

**Procedure:**

Juice all ingredients, combining them in your juicer one at a time.

If blending, add all ingredients to a blender with water or apple juice for smoother consistency. Blend and then strain.

Enjoy immediately, served over ice if preferred, for a sweet and earthy nutrient-rich drink.

**N.V.:** Rich in antioxidants, boosts stamina, and supports liver detoxification.

## Recipe 3: Sweet Potato Sunrise

**P.T.:** 7 minutes

**Ingr.:**

1 large sweet potato, peeled and chopped

2 large carrots, peeled and chopped

Juice of 1 orange

1/2 inch piece of ginger, peeled

**Servings:** 2

**M.C.:** Juicing

**Procedure:**

Pass the sweet potato, carrots, and ginger through a juicer.

Stir in the orange juice to the extracted juice for added sweetness and vitamin C.

Serve the juice immediately, or chill for a refreshing and energizing drink.

**N.V.:** High in beta-carotene, vitamins A and C, and a good source of magnesium. Ginger adds anti-inflammatory properties.

## Recipe 4: Turnip Twister

**P.T.:** 5 minutes

**Ingr.:**

2 medium turnips, peeled and chopped

1 pear, cored and sliced

Juice of 1 lemon

A handful of fresh mint leaves

**Servings:** 2

**M.C.:** Juicing

**Procedure:**

Combine turnips, pear, and lemon juice in a juicer.

After juicing, stir in mint leaves for a refreshing flavor.

Serve immediately for a digestive-friendly, nutrient-packed juice.

**N.V.:** Rich in vitamin C, digestive enzymes, and antioxidants. Mint promotes digestion and adds a fresh aftertaste.

## Recipe 5: Radish Refresher

**P.T.:** 6 minutes

**Ingr.:**

1 cup radishes, trimmed and halved

1 large cucumber, peeled and chopped

Juice of 2 limes

1 teaspoon honey (optional)

**Servings:** 2

**M.C.:** Juicing

**Procedure:**

Juice the radishes and cucumber together.

Stir in the lime juice and honey for a balance of spicy and sweet.

Serve chilled for a hydrating and spicy detox juice.

**N.V.:** Provides hydration, vitamin C, and potassium. Radishes are also known for their detoxifying properties.

## Recipe 6: Parsnip Pear Potion

**P.T.:** 5 minutes

**Ingr.:**

2 parsnips, peeled and chopped

2 pears, cored and sliced

A pinch of nutmeg

1/2 cup water (for blending, if needed)

**Servings:** 2

**M.C.:** Juicing/Blending

**Procedure:**

Juice or blend parsnips and pears together, depending on your equipment.

If blending, add water to achieve desired consistency.

Stir in a pinch of nutmeg for a hint of warmth.

Serve immediately to enjoy a naturally sweet and slightly spiced juice.

**N.V.:** High in fiber, vitamins C and K, and potassium. Nutmeg adds a soothing effect and can aid digestion.

## Recipe 7: Spicy Gingered Carrot

**P.T.:** 5 minutes

**Ingr.:**

5 carrots, peeled and chopped

1 inch piece of ginger, peeled

1 apple, cored and sliced

A pinch of cayenne pepper

**Servings:** 2

**M.C.:** Juicing

**Procedure:**

Juice the carrots, ginger, and apple together.

Stir in a pinch of cayenne pepper for a metabolic boost.

Serve immediately for a kick of spice and a boost of energy.

**N.V.:** Loaded with vitamin A, aids in digestion and metabolism. The ginger and cayenne pepper have anti-inflammatory and thermogenic properties, respectively.

## Recipe 8: Celery Root Citrus Blast

**P.T.:** 8 minutes

**Ingr.:**

1 celery root (celeriac), peeled and chopped

2 oranges, peeled and sectioned

1 carrot, peeled and chopped

Juice of 1 lemon

**Servings:** 2

**M.C.:** Juicing

**Procedure:**

Juice celery root, oranges, carrot, and lemon together.

Serve the juice immediately, ensuring a vibrant, nutrient-rich drink.

**N.V.:** High in vitamin C, potassium, and antioxidants. Celery root provides a unique flavor and aids in digestion and detoxification.

## Recipe 9: Golden Beet Elixir

**P.T.:** 10 minutes
**Ingr.:**
2 golden beets, peeled and chopped
2 carrots, peeled and chopped
1 apple, cored and sliced
1/2 teaspoon turmeric powder
**Servings:** 2
**M.C.:** Juicing
**Procedure:**
Juice the golden beets, carrots, and apple.
Stir in turmeric powder for additional anti-inflammatory benefits.
Serve chilled for a sweet, earthy, and health-boosting juice.
**N.V.:** Offers a good source of folate, manganese, and is anti-inflammatory. Turmeric adds curcumin, a powerful antioxidant.

# Nightshade Vegetable Juices

## Recipe 1: Tomato Tango Detox

**P.T.:** 5 minutes
**Ingr.:**
4 large tomatoes, chopped
1 red bell pepper, deseeded and chopped
1 small cucumber, chopped
2 stalks of celery, chopped
Juice of 1 lemon
A pinch of sea salt
A dash of cayenne pepper (optional)
**Servings:** 2
**M.C.:** Blending
**Procedure:**
Place all the vegetables in a blender and add lemon juice.
Blend until smooth. For a thinner consistency, you can add a little water.
Season with sea salt and cayenne pepper to taste.
Strain the mixture through a fine mesh sieve for a smoother juice, if desired.
Serve chilled for a refreshing and detoxifying drink.
**N.V.:** High in vitamins A, C, and K, antioxidants, and hydration. Cayenne pepper adds a metabolic boost.

## Recipe 2: Spicy Eggplant Elixir

**P.T.:** 10 minutes

**Ingr.:**

1 medium eggplant, roasted and skin removed

2 tomatoes, chopped

1 carrot, chopped

1/2 inch piece of ginger, peeled

1 garlic clove

Juice of 1 lime

Salt and black pepper to taste

**Servings:** 2

**M.C.:** Blending

**Procedure:**

Roast the eggplant in the oven until tender, let cool, then peel off the skin.

Place the roasted eggplant, tomatoes, carrot, ginger, and garlic in a blender.

Add lime juice for a tangy flavor.

Blend until smooth, adding a bit of water if necessary for the desired consistency.

Season with salt and pepper.

Serve the juice immediately, or chilled, as a unique savory treat.

**N.V.:** Rich in dietary fiber, vitamins B and C, potassium, and antioxidants. Ginger and garlic add anti-inflammatory and immune-boosting properties.

## Recipe 3: Peppery Potato Punch

**P.T.:** 10 minutes (excluding cooling time)

**Ingr.:**

1 large potato, boiled and cooled

1 green bell pepper, chopped

A handful of parsley, chopped

Juice of 1 lemon

1 cup of water

Salt, to taste

**Servings:** 2

**M.C.:** Blending

**Procedure:**

Peel the boiled potato and place it in a blender.

Add the green bell pepper, parsley, lemon juice, and water.

Blend until smooth. Add more water if a thinner consistency is preferred.

Season with salt to taste.

Serve chilled for a nutrient-dense, savory juice.

**N.V.:** High in vitamin C, B vitamins, and potassium. The parsley provides iron and the lemon juice enhances iron absorption.

## Recipe 4: Chili Pepper Power Shot

**P.T.:** 5 minutes

**Ingr.:**

2 red chili peppers, seeds removed

2 tomatoes, chopped

1 small apple, cored and sliced

A pinch of salt

**Servings:** 2 small shots

**M.C.:** Juicing

**Procedure:**

Carefully deseed the chili peppers to adjust the heat level according to preference.

Pass the chili peppers, tomatoes, and apple through a juicer.

Add a pinch of salt to enhance the flavors.

Serve immediately in shot glasses for a spicy, energizing boost.

**N.V.:** A great source of vitamin C and capsaicin, which boosts metabolism.

## Recipe 5: Bell Pepper Bliss

**P.T.:** 8 minutes

**Ingr.:**

1 red bell pepper, chopped

1 yellow bell pepper, chopped

1 orange bell pepper, chopped

Juice of 2 oranges

1 carrot, chopped

**Servings:** 2

**M.C.:** Juicing

**Procedure:**

Juice all the bell peppers, oranges, and carrot together.

Mix well to ensure the flavors are well combined.

Serve this vibrant, nutrient-packed juice immediately, or chilled.

**N.V.:** Full of vitamins A, C, and E, along with antioxidants that support immune health.

## Recipe 6: Solanum Smoothie

**P.T.:** 10 minutes

**Ingr.:**

1 small beetroot, peeled and chopped

1 cooked sweet potato, peeled

A dash of turmeric powder

1 cup almond milk or water for blending

**Servings:** 2

**M.C.:** Blending

**Procedure:**

Combine beetroot, sweet potato, turmeric, and almond milk in a blender.

Blend until smooth. If the mixture is too thick, add more almond milk or water to reach the desired consistency.

Serve immediately for a creamy, earthy smoothie full of antioxidants and anti-inflammatory benefits.

**N.V.:** High in fiber, potassium, and vitamins A and C. Turmeric adds anti-inflammatory properties.

## Recipe 7: Tomatillo Twist

**P.T.:** 7 minutes

**Ingr.:**

4 tomatillos, husked and chopped

1/2 cucumber, chopped

Juice of 2 limes

1/4 jalapeño, seeded (optional for extra heat)

1/2 cup of water

**Servings:** 2

**M.C.:** Blending

**Procedure:**

Place tomatillos, cucumber, lime juice, jalapeño (if using), and water in a blender.

Blend until smooth; add more water if needed for desired consistency.

Serve chilled for a tangy, refreshing drink with a kick.

**N.V.:** Rich in vitamin C, dietary fiber, and antioxidants. Jalapeño provides metabolism-boosting capsaicin.

## Recipe 8: Savory Solanaceae Squeeze

**P.T.:** 10 minutes

**Ingr.:**

2 medium tomatoes, chopped

1 red bell pepper, deseeded and chopped

1 small red onion, peeled and quartered

A handful of fresh oregano leaves

Salt and pepper to taste

1 cup of vegetable broth (for a savory twist)

**Servings:** 2

**M.C.:** Blending

**Procedure:**

Combine tomatoes, red bell pepper, red onion, and oregano in a blender.

Add the vegetable broth to bring a savory depth to the juice.

Blend until smooth. For a thinner consistency, additional broth or water can be added.

Season with salt and pepper according to taste.

Serve chilled or at room temperature as a refreshing, savory juice.

**N.V.:** Rich in vitamins A, C, and E, antioxidants, and flavonoids. The addition of vegetable broth provides a comforting, umami flavor and additional nutrients.

## Recipe 9: Aubergine Dream

**P.T.:** 15 minutes (including roasting time)

**Ingr.:**

1 large eggplant (aubergine), roasted and peeled

1 clove of garlic, minced

Juice of 1 lemon

1 tablespoon tahini (sesame paste)

1 cup water or vegetable broth

Salt and smoked paprika to taste

**Servings:** 2

**M.C.:** Blending

**Procedure:**

Roast the eggplant in the oven at 400°F (200°C) until the skin is charred and the inside is tender, about 10-15 minutes. Allow to cool, then peel.

In a blender, combine the roasted eggplant flesh, minced garlic, lemon juice, and tahini. Add water or vegetable broth to reach your desired consistency.

Blend until smooth, then season with salt and smoked paprika.

Serve this unique, savory juice chilled or at room temperature, garnished with a sprinkle of paprika.

**N.V.:** High in dietary fiber, potassium, and vitamins B1 and B6. Tahini adds calcium and healthy fats.

## Recipe 10: Daikon Digestive Tonic

**P.T.:** 7 minutes

**Ingr.:**

1 large daikon radish, peeled and chopped

1 pear, cored and sliced

A handful of fresh mint leaves

Juice of 1 lemon

1/2 inch piece of ginger, peeled and minced

1/2 cup of water or coconut water

**Servings:** 2

**M.C.:** Blending

**Procedure:**

Place the daikon radish, pear, mint leaves, lemon juice, ginger, and water or coconut water in a blender.

Blend until smooth. If the mixture is too thick, add more water or coconut water.

Taste and adjust the sweetness or mintiness as desired.

Serve chilled for a refreshing and digestive-aiding beverage.

**N.V.:** Excellent source of vitamin C, aids in digestion, and acts as a natural diuretic. Ginger and mint provide soothing gastrointestinal benefits.

# Bitter and Savory Options

## Recipe 1: Bitter Greens Tonic

**P.T.:** 5 minutes

**Ingr.:**

1 cup kale, chopped

1 cup dandelion greens, chopped

1 small cucumber, sliced

Juice of 1 lemon

1 inch turmeric root, peeled

1 teaspoon apple cider vinegar

1 cup water

**Servings:** 2

**M.C.:** Blending

**Procedure:**

Combine kale, dandelion greens, cucumber, lemon juice, turmeric root, and apple cider vinegar in a blender.

Add water and blend until smooth.

Strain the mixture through a fine mesh sieve for a smoother texture, if desired.

Serve immediately, garnished with a slice of lemon.

**N.V.:** Rich in vitamins A, C, and K, iron, and antioxidants. Turmeric and apple cider vinegar add anti-inflammatory and digestive benefits.

## Recipe 2: Savory Beet Broth

**P.T.:** 10 minutes

**Ingr.:**

2 medium beets, peeled and chopped

1 carrot, peeled and chopped

1 celery stalk, chopped

2 cups vegetable broth

1 bay leaf

Salt and pepper to taste

**Servings:** 2

**M.C.:** Simmering

**Procedure:**

Combine all ingredients in a large pot and bring to a simmer over medium heat.

Cook for 10 minutes, allowing the flavors to meld.

Remove from heat and let cool slightly. Remove the bay leaf.

Blend the mixture until smooth. Strain if desired for a clearer broth.

Adjust seasoning with salt and pepper.

Serve warm or chilled, according to preference.

**N.V.:** High in fiber, folate, and vitamins A and C. The vegetable broth base adds a comforting, savory depth.

## Recipe 3: Cabbage Cure

**P.T.:** 5 minutes

**Ingr.:**

2 cups green cabbage, chopped

1/2 cup aloe vera juice

1 pear, cored and sliced

**Servings:** 2

**M.C.:** Juicing

**Procedure:**

Juice the green cabbage and pear together.

Stir in the aloe vera juice until well combined.

Serve chilled to benefit from its digestive soothing properties.

**N.V.:** Rich in vitamins C and K, aids in digestion and hydration, with anti-inflammatory benefits from aloe vera.

## Recipe 4: Fennel Freshness

**P.T.:** 7 minutes

**Ingr.:**

1 large fennel bulb, chopped

1 green apple, cored and sliced

A handful of fresh mint leaves

**Servings:** 2

**M.C.:** Blending

**Procedure:**

Blend fennel, green apple, and mint leaves with a cup of water until smooth.

Strain the blend for a smoother texture, if preferred.

Serve immediately for a refreshingly crisp juice.

**N.V.:** Excellent source of vitamin C, fiber, and potent antioxidants. Mint adds a digestive aid.

## Recipe 5: Bitter Melon Magic

**P.T.:** 8 minutes

**Ingr.:**

1 bitter melon, seeds removed and chopped

1 cucumber, chopped

Juice of 1 lemon

**Servings:** 2

**M.C.:** Juicing

**Procedure:**

Pass the bitter melon and cucumber through a juicer.

Stir in the lemon juice for a balancing citrus note.

Serve immediately, ideally on an empty stomach for detox benefits.

**N.V.:** A powerhouse of antioxidants, known to lower blood sugar levels and improve digestive health.

## Recipe 6: Savory Tomato Sip

**P.T.:** 10 minutes

**Ingr.:**

4 ripe tomatoes, chopped

1 red bell pepper, chopped

1 clove garlic

A handful of fresh basil leaves

**Servings:** 2

**M.C.:** Blending

**Procedure:**

Combine tomatoes, red bell pepper, garlic, and basil in a blender.

Blend until smooth, adding a little water if necessary for consistency.

Season with salt and pepper to taste.

Serve chilled as a nutritious, soup-like juice.

**N.V.:** Loaded with lycopene, vitamin C, and antioxidants. Basil provides anti-inflammatory properties.

## Recipe 7: Kale and Kombu Drink

**P.T.:** 15 minutes (including soaking time for kombu)

**Ingr.:**

2 cups kale, chopped

1 piece of kombu (seaweed), soaked and chopped

1 teaspoon soy sauce

1 cup water

**Servings:** 2

**M.C.:** Blending

**Procedure:**

Soak kombu in water for about 10 minutes to soften.

Blend soaked kombu, kale, soy sauce, and water until smooth.

Serve immediately for a mineral-rich, umami-packed green juice.

**N.V.:** High in vitamins A, C, K, iodine, and minerals. Soy sauce adds depth and umami.

## Recipe 8: Radish Detoxifier

**P.T.:** 5 minutes

**Ingr.:**

1 cup radishes, chopped

1/2 cup parsley, chopped

Juice of 1 lemon

**Servings:** 2

**M.C.:** Juicing

**Procedure:**

Juice radishes and parsley together.

Stir in lemon juice and serve chilled.

**N.V.:** Supports detoxification, rich in vitamin C, and has anti-cancer properties.

## Recipe 9: Gingered Greens

**P.T.:** 7 minutes

**Ingr.:**

2 cups spinach

1/2 cup parsley

1 inch piece of ginger, peeled

2 stalks of celery

**Servings:** 2

**M.C.:** Juicing

**Procedure:**

Pass all ingredients through a juicer.

Serve the juice immediately for an energizing and immune-boosting effect.

**N.V.:** High in iron, vitamins A and C, and promotes digestion and anti-inflammatory benefits.

# 7. The World of Smoothies

## Basic Smoothie Building Blocks

### Recipe 1: Classic Berry Banana Smoothie

**P.T.:** 5 minutes

**Ingr.:**

1 banana, peeled and sliced

1/2 cup mixed berries (strawberries, blueberries, raspberries)

1 cup almond milk

1 tablespoon chia seeds

A handful of spinach (optional for added nutrients)

**Servings:** 1

**M.C.:** Blending

**Procedure:**

Place the banana, mixed berries, almond milk, chia seeds, and spinach (if using) into a blender.

Blend on high until smooth and creamy.

Serve immediately for a refreshing and nutritious smoothie.

**N.V.:** High in fiber, antioxidants, Omega-3 fatty acids, vitamins, and minerals.

### Recipe 2: Green Power Smoothie

**P.T.:** 5 minutes

**Ingr.:**

1 cup fresh spinach

1/2 avocado, pitted and scooped

1/2 apple, cored and sliced

1 tablespoon flaxseed meal

1 cup coconut water

Juice of 1/2 lemon

**Servings:** 1

**M.C.:** Blending

**Procedure:**

Combine spinach, avocado, apple, flaxseed meal, coconut water, and lemon juice in a blender.

Blend until smooth.

Enjoy immediately for a boost of energy and nutrients.

**N.V.:** Rich in healthy fats, hydration, fiber, vitamins A and C, and potassium.

### Recipe 3: Tropical Mango Sunrise

**P.T.:** 5 minutes

**Ingr.:**

1 ripe mango, peeled and cubed

1/2 cup pineapple chunks

1 cup coconut milk

1 teaspoon turmeric powder

Ice cubes (optional)

**Servings:** 1-2

**M.C.:** Blending

**Procedure:**

Place the mango, pineapple, coconut milk, and turmeric in a blender.

Add ice cubes if a colder consistency is desired.

Blend until smooth and creamy.

Serve immediately for a refreshing, anti-inflammatory boost.

**N.V.:** Rich in vitamins A and C, anti-inflammatory properties from turmeric, and healthy fats from coconut milk.

## Recipe 4: Peanut Butter Banana Protein

**P.T.:** 5 minutes

**Ingr.:**

1 large banana

2 tablespoons peanut butter

1/2 cup Greek yogurt

1 cup almond milk

1 tablespoon honey (optional)

**Servings:** 1-2

**M.C.:** Blending

**Procedure:**

Combine the banana, peanut butter, Greek yogurt, almond milk, and honey in a blender. Blend until smooth.

Serve immediately for a protein-rich, energizing smoothie.

**N.V.:** High in protein, potassium, and healthy fats. Excellent for post-workout recovery.

## Recipe 5: Antioxidant Acai Bowl

**P.T.:** 10 minutes

**Ingr.:**

1 packet frozen acai berry puree

1 banana, sliced

1/2 cup mixed berries

1/4 cup apple juice

Granola, sliced fruit, and honey for topping

**Servings:** 1

**M.C.:** Blending

**Procedure:**

Blend the acai puree, half of the banana, mixed berries, and apple juice until smooth.

Pour into a bowl and top with granola, the remaining banana slices, and a drizzle of honey.

Serve immediately as a nutrient-dense breakfast or snack.

**N.V.:** Loaded with antioxidants, fiber, and vitamins. A healthy, energizing meal option.

## Recipe 6: Chocolate Avocado Bliss

**P.T.:** 5 minutes

**Ingr.:**

1/2 ripe avocado

2 tablespoons cocoa powder

1 banana

2 tablespoons honey or maple syrup

1 cup milk (any variety)

**Servings:** 1-2

**M.C.:** Blending

**Procedure:**

Add avocado, cocoa powder, banana, honey/maple syrup, and milk to a blender. Blend until creamy and smooth.

Serve immediately for a decadent yet healthy treat.

**N.V.:** Offers healthy fats, magnesium, and mood-boosting compounds from cocoa.

### Recipe 7: Oatmeal Breakfast Smoothie

**P.T.:** 5 minutes

**Ingr.:**

1/2 cup rolled oats

1 banana

1 tablespoon almond butter

1 cup almond milk

A dash of cinnamon

**Servings:** 1-2

**M.C.:** Blending

**Procedure:**

Soak oats in almond milk for 5 minutes to soften.

Add soaked oats, banana, almond butter, and cinnamon to a blender.

Blend until smooth.

Serve for a filling, nutritious breakfast smoothie.

**N.V.:** High in fiber, protein, and essential minerals. Provides sustained energy.

### Recipe 8: Super Seed Smoothie

**P.T.:** 5 minutes

**Ingr.:**

1 tablespoon chia seeds

1 tablespoon flaxseed meal

1 tablespoon hemp seeds

1 cup mixed berries

Juice of 1 orange

**Servings:** 1-2

**M.C.:** Blending

**Procedure:**

Mix chia seeds, flaxseed meal, hemp seeds, mixed berries, and orange juice in a blender. Blend until smooth.

Serve immediately to enjoy a smoothie packed with omega-3 fatty acids and antioxidants.

**N.V.:** Rich in omega-3 fatty acids, fiber, and vitamin C. Supports heart health and digestion.

### Recipe 9: Detox Green Machine

**P.T.:** 5 minutes

**Ingr.:**

2 cups kale or spinach

1/2 cucumber

1 green apple, cored and sliced

Juice of 1/2 lemon

1 inch piece of ginger, peeled

1 cup coconut water

**Servings:** 1-2

**M.C.:** Blending

**Procedure:**

Combine all ingredients in a blender.

Blend until smooth.

Serve immediately for a detoxifying and energizing green smoothie.

**N.V.:** High in vitamins A, C, and K, electrolytes from coconut water, and digestive aids from ginger.

# Protein-Packed Recipes

## Recipe 1: Vanilla Almond Protein Shake

**P.T.:** 5 minutes

**Ingr.:**

1 cup unsweetened almond milk

1 ripe banana, frozen

2 tablespoons almond butter

1 scoop vanilla protein powder (whey or plant-based)

1/2 teaspoon cinnamon

A handful of ice cubes

**Servings:** 1

**M.C.:** Blending

**Procedure:**

Place almond milk, frozen banana, almond butter, vanilla protein powder, and cinnamon in a blender.

Add ice cubes to achieve your desired thickness.

Blend on high until smooth and creamy.

Pour into a glass and serve immediately for a nourishing, protein-rich smoothie.

**N.V.:** High in protein, healthy fats, and fiber. Provides energy and supports muscle recovery.

## Recipe 2: Berry Spinach Power Smoothie

**P.T.:** 5 minutes

**Ingr.:**

1 cup fresh spinach leaves

1 cup mixed berries (strawberries, blueberries, raspberries), fresh or frozen

1 cup Greek yogurt, plain

1 tablespoon chia seeds

1 scoop protein powder (any flavor that complements berries)

1/2 cup water or almond milk, as needed for blending

**Servings:** 1

**M.C.:** Blending

**Procedure:**

Combine spinach, mixed berries, Greek yogurt, chia seeds, and protein powder in a blender.

Add water or almond milk to help blend, depending on your preferred consistency.

Blend until smooth, ensuring the spinach and berries are fully incorporated.

Serve in a tall glass for a refreshing, protein-packed meal or snack.

**N.V.:** Rich in protein, antioxidants, omega-3 fatty acids, and vitamins. Excellent for post-workout recovery or a meal replacement.

### Recipe 3: Spinach Avocado Protein Smoothie

**P.T.:** 5 minutes

**Ingr.:**

1 cup fresh spinach leaves

1/2 ripe avocado

1 scoop vanilla protein powder

1 cup unsweetened almond milk

Juice of 1/2 lemon

Ice cubes (optional)

**Servings:** 1

**M.C.:** Blending

**Procedure:**

Add the spinach, avocado, protein powder, almond milk, and lemon juice into a blender.

Blend on high until smooth. Add ice cubes for a colder, thicker smoothie.

Serve immediately, garnishing with a slice of lemon if desired.

**N.V.:** Rich in healthy fats, fiber, protein, and vitamins A and C. Lemon juice adds a refreshing zing and aids in iron absorption from spinach.

### Recipe 4: Mocha Morning Boost

**P.T.:** 5 minutes

**Ingr.:**

1 scoop chocolate protein powder

1 cup cold brew coffee

1/2 ripe banana

1/2 cup Greek yogurt

Ice cubes

**Servings:** 1

**M.C.:** Blending

**Procedure:**

Combine the protein powder, cold brew coffee, banana, Greek yogurt, and ice cubes in a blender.

Blend until creamy and smooth.

Pour into a glass and enjoy a protein-packed start to your day with an energizing coffee kick.

**N.V.:** Provides caffeine for energy, protein for muscle repair, and potassium from the banana.

## Recipe 5: Tropical Hemp Seed Smoothie

**P.T.:** 5 minutes

**Ingr.:**

1 cup pineapple chunks

1 ripe banana

1 tablespoon hemp seeds

1 scoop vanilla protein powder

1 cup coconut water

**Servings:** 1

**M.C.:** Blending

**Procedure:**

Place pineapple, banana, hemp seeds, protein powder, and coconut water in a blender.

Blend until smooth and fully combined.

Serve chilled for a refreshing, protein-rich tropical treat.

**N.V.:** High in protein, omega-3 fatty acids, and electrolytes, making it perfect for hydration and recovery.

## Recipe 6: Almond Joy Protein Shake

**P.T.:** 5 minutes

**Ingr.:**

1 scoop chocolate protein powder

2 tablespoons almond butter

1 cup unsweetened almond milk

A handful of unsweetened coconut flakes

Ice cubes

**Servings:** 1

**M.C.:** Blending

**Procedure:**

Add all ingredients to a blender, finishing with ice cubes.

Blend until creamy.

Enjoy the flavors of an Almond Joy candy bar in a healthy, protein-packed smoothie.

**N.V.:** Rich in protein and healthy fats from almond butter, plus fiber from coconut flakes.

## Recipe 7: Pumpkin Pie Protein Smoothie

**P.T.:** 5 minutes

**Ingr.:**

1/2 cup pumpkin puree

1 scoop vanilla protein powder

1/2 teaspoon pumpkin pie spice

1 cup Greek yogurt

A drizzle of honey (optional)

**Servings:** 1

**M.C.:** Blending

**Procedure:**

Combine pumpkin puree, protein powder, pumpkin pie spice, Greek yogurt, and honey in a blender.

Blend until smooth.

Serve immediately, enjoying the taste of fall in every sip.

**N.V.:** Packed with protein, fiber, and vitamins A and C. The spices add anti-inflammatory benefits.

## Recipe 8: Blueberry Oatmeal Protein Smoothie

**P.T.:** 5 minutes

**Ingr.:**

1 cup blueberries (fresh or frozen)

1/2 cup rolled oats

1 scoop vanilla protein powder

1 cup almond milk

A dash of cinnamon

**Servings:** 1

**M.C.:** Blending

**Procedure:**

Soak the rolled oats in almond milk for 5 minutes to soften.

Add soaked oats, blueberries, protein powder, and cinnamon to a blender.

Blend until smooth.

Enjoy a hearty, nutritious smoothie perfect for breakfast or a post-workout snack.

**N.V.:** Offers sustained energy from oats, antioxidants from blueberries, and muscle-repairing protein.

## Recipe 9: Apple Cinnamon Protein Smoothie

**P.T.:** 5 minutes

**Ingr.:**

1 apple, cored and sliced

1 scoop vanilla protein powder

1 cup Greek yogurt

A dash of cinnamon

1 tablespoon almond butter

**Servings:** 1

**M.C.:** Blending

**Procedure:**

Combine the apple, protein powder, Greek yogurt, cinnamon, and almond butter in a blender.

Blend until smooth.

Serve chilled for a smoothie that's both nutritious and reminiscent of apple pie.

**N.V.:** High in protein and fiber, with a boost of healthy fats from almond butter. Cinnamon adds blood sugar regulation properties.

# Breakfast Smoothie Ideas

## Recipe 1: Sunrise Berry Oat Smoothie

**P.T.:** 5 minutes

**Ingr.:**

1 cup mixed berries (strawberries, blueberries, raspberries), fresh or frozen

1/2 cup rolled oats

1 banana

1 tablespoon almond butter

1 cup almond milk

1 teaspoon chia seeds

**Servings:** 2

**M.C.:** Blending

**Procedure:**

Combine berries, oats, banana, almond butter, almond milk, and chia seeds in a blender.

Blend until smooth. If the mixture is too thick, add more almond milk to achieve desired consistency.

Serve immediately for a fiber-rich, energizing breakfast.

**N.V.:** High in dietary fiber, omega-3 fatty acids, vitamins, and minerals. Provides sustained energy and aids in digestion.

## Recipe 2: Green Protein Power Smoothie

**P.T.:** 5 minutes

**Ingr.:**

2 cups spinach leaves

1 ripe avocado, peeled and pitted

1/2 cup Greek yogurt

1 scoop vanilla protein powder

1 cup coconut water

Juice of 1 lime

**Servings:** 2

**M.C.:** Blending

**Procedure:**

Place spinach, avocado, Greek yogurt, protein powder, coconut water, and lime juice into a blender.

Blend until creamy and smooth.

Serve chilled for a nutritious, protein-packed start to your day.

**N.V.:** Rich in protein, healthy fats, vitamins A and C, calcium, and iron. Supports muscle recovery and hydration.

## Recipe 3: Nutty Banana Flax Smoothie

**P.T.:** 5 minutes

**Ingr.:**

2 ripe bananas

2 tablespoons natural peanut butter

1 tablespoon ground flaxseed

1 cup unsweetened soy milk (or any milk of choice)

A dash of cinnamon

**Servings:** 2

**M.C.:** Blending

**Procedure:**

Combine bananas, peanut butter, ground flaxseed, soy milk, and cinnamon in a blender.

Blend until smooth and creamy.

Serve immediately for a filling and nutritious breakfast smoothie.

**N.V.:** High in protein, omega-3 fatty acids from flaxseed, potassium from bananas, and antioxidants from cinnamon.

## Recipe 4: Tropical Mango Coconut Smoothie

**P.T.:** 5 minutes

**Ingr.:**

1 cup frozen mango chunks

1/2 cup Greek yogurt

1 cup coconut milk

Juice of 1 lime

**Servings:** 2

**M.C.:** Blending

**Procedure:**

Add mango chunks, Greek yogurt, coconut milk, and lime juice to a blender.

Blend until smooth and well combined.

Serve chilled for a creamy, tropical smoothie that's perfect for a refreshing start.

**N.V.:** Rich in vitamin C, probiotics from Greek yogurt, and healthy fats from coconut milk.

## Recipe 5: Berry Beet Detox Smoothie

**P.T.:** 5 minutes

**Ingr.:**

1 small cooked beet, peeled and chopped

1 cup frozen mixed berries

1/2 apple, cored and chopped

1 tablespoon lemon juice

1 cup water or coconut water

**Servings:** 2

**M.C.:** Blending

**Procedure:**

Place beet, mixed berries, apple, lemon juice, and water/coconut water in a blender.

Blend until smooth.

Enjoy a vibrant, nutrient-packed smoothie that supports detoxification and boosts energy.

**N.V.:** Loaded with antioxidants, fiber, and vitamins. Beet enhances liver detoxification.

## Recipe 6: Peanut Butter Oatmeal Smoothie

**P.T.:** 5 minutes

**Ingr.:**

1/2 cup rolled oats

2 tablespoons peanut butter

1 large ripe banana

1 cup almond milk

1 tablespoon honey or maple syrup (optional)

**Servings:** 2

**M.C.:** Blending

**Procedure:**

Add rolled oats to a blender and pulse until they're a fine powder.

Add peanut butter, banana, almond milk, and sweetener if using. Blend until smooth.

Serve for a breakfast smoothie that keeps you full and satisfied.

**N.V.:** Offers sustained energy from oats, protein and healthy fats from peanut butter, and natural sweetness from banana.

## Recipe 7: Kale Pineapple Ginger Smoothie

**P.T.:** 5 minutes

**Ingr.:**

2 cups kale, stems removed

1 cup frozen pineapple chunks

1/2 inch ginger, peeled

1 banana

1 cup water or coconut water

**Servings:** 2

**M.C.:** Blending

**Procedure:**

Combine kale, pineapple, ginger, banana, and water/coconut water in a blender.

Blend until smooth and creamy.

Serve immediately for a zingy, energizing breakfast option.

**N.V.:** High in vitamin A, vitamin C, and potassium. Ginger adds digestive benefits.

## Recipe 8: Chocolate Avocado Smoothie

**P.T.:** 5 minutes

**Ingr.:**

1 ripe avocado

2 tablespoons cocoa powder

1 banana

1 cup milk (choice)

Sweetener to taste (honey, maple syrup, or stevia)

**Servings:** 2

**M.C.:** Blending

**Procedure:**

Scoop out the avocado and place it in the blender with the cocoa powder, banana, milk, and sweetener.

Blend until creamy.

Enjoy a rich, creamy smoothie that's both nutritious and indulgent.

**N.V.:** Avocado provides healthy fats and fiber, while cocoa adds antioxidants without the sugar of chocolate.

### Recipe 9: Apple Pie Smoothie

**P.T.:** 5 minutes

**Ingr.:**

1 large apple, cored and chopped

1/4 cup rolled oats

1/2 cup Greek yogurt

1 cup almond milk

Dash of cinnamon and nutmeg

**Servings:** 2

**M.C.:** Blending

**Procedure:**

Add apple, oats, Greek yogurt, almond milk, cinnamon, and nutmeg to a blender.

Blend until smooth.

Serve for a breakfast smoothie that captures the essence of apple pie.

**N.V.:** High in fiber, probiotics from Greek yogurt, and spices that regulate blood sugar levels.

## Dessert-Inspired Creations

### Recipe 1: Chocolate Hazelnut Heaven

**P.T.:** 5 minutes

**Ingr.:**

2 tablespoons hazelnut butter

1 ripe banana

2 tablespoons cocoa powder

1 cup almond milk

1 scoop chocolate protein powder (optional for a protein boost)

Ice cubes

**Servings:** 1-2

**M.C.:** Blending

**Procedure:**

Combine hazelnut butter, banana, cocoa powder, almond milk, and chocolate protein powder in a blender.

Add ice cubes to achieve desired consistency.

Blend until smooth and creamy.

Serve immediately, garnished with a sprinkle of cocoa powder or shaved dark chocolate.

**N.V.:** Rich in healthy fats from hazelnut butter, antioxidants from cocoa, and protein if protein powder is used.

## Recipe 2: Key Lime Pie Smoothie

**P.T.:** 5 minutes

**Ingr.:**

Juice of 4 key limes

1 ripe avocado

1/2 cup Greek yogurt

2 tablespoons honey or agave syrup

1/2 teaspoon vanilla extract

1 cup ice cubes

Graham cracker crumbs for garnish (optional)

**Servings:** 1-2

**M.C.:** Blending

**Procedure:**

Add key lime juice, avocado, Greek yogurt, honey/agave syrup, vanilla extract, and ice cubes to a blender.

Blend until smooth and creamy.

Pour into glasses and sprinkle with graham cracker crumbs if desired.

Serve immediately for a refreshing take on the classic dessert.

**N.V.:** High in vitamins C and E from avocado, protein from Greek yogurt, and natural sweetness.

## Recipe 3: Apple Crisp Smoothie

**P.T.:** 5 minutes

**Ingr.:**

1 large apple, cored and chopped

1/4 cup rolled oats

1/2 cup vanilla almond milk

A dash of cinnamon

1 tablespoon maple syrup

Ice cubes

**Servings:** 1-2

**M.C.:** Blending

**Procedure:**

Place the apple, rolled oats, vanilla almond milk, cinnamon, maple syrup, and ice cubes into a blender.

Blend on high until smooth and creamy.

Serve in a glass with an additional sprinkle of cinnamon on top for garnish.

**N.V.:** This smoothie is high in dietary fiber, vitamins, and minerals from the apple and oats, with a comforting cinnamon flavor that mimics apple crisp dessert.

## Recipe 4: Pumpkin Spice Latte Smoothie

**P.T.:** 5 minutes

**Ingr.:**

1/2 cup pumpkin puree (canned or fresh)

1 cup cold brew coffee

1/2 cup almond milk

1 teaspoon pumpkin pie spice

Sweetener of choice to taste

Ice cubes

**Servings:** 1-2

**M.C.:** Blending

**Procedure:**

Add the pumpkin puree, cold brew coffee, almond milk, pumpkin pie spice, sweetener, and ice cubes to a blender.

Blend until smooth and well combined.

Serve chilled, topped with a sprinkle of pumpkin pie spice or whipped cream for an extra treat.

**N.V.:** Offers a boost of vitamins A and C from the pumpkin, with the spice blend providing anti-inflammatory benefits.

## Recipe 5: Blueberry Cheesecake Smoothie

**P.T.:** 5 minutes

**Ingr.:**

1 cup frozen blueberries

1/2 cup cottage cheese or Greek yogurt

1/2 ripe banana

1 tablespoon honey or maple syrup

1/4 cup almond milk

**Servings:** 1-2

**M.C.:** Blending

**Procedure:**

Combine blueberries, cottage cheese/Greek yogurt, banana, honey/maple syrup, and almond milk in a blender.

Blend until smooth and creamy.

Pour into glasses and serve, mimicking the rich taste of a blueberry cheesecake.

**N.V.:** Rich in antioxidants from blueberries, protein from cottage cheese or Greek yogurt, and natural sweetness from honey.

## Recipe 6: Peanut Butter Cup Smoothie

**P.T.:** 5 minutes

**Ingr.:**

2 tablespoons natural peanut butter

1 ripe banana

2 tablespoons unsweetened cocoa powder

1 cup milk of choice (e.g., almond, soy, dairy)

1 tablespoon honey or to taste

Ice cubes

**Servings:** 1-2

**M.C.:** Blending

**Procedure:**

Place peanut butter, banana, cocoa powder, milk, honey, and ice cubes in a blender.

Blend until smooth and creamy, adjusting sweetness to taste.

Serve with a drizzle of peanut butter on top for a decadent treat.

**N.V.:** High in protein and healthy fats from the peanut butter, with mood-boosting magnesium from cocoa powder.

## Recipe 7: Strawberry Shortcake Smoothie

**P.T.:** 5 minutes

**Ingr.:**

1 cup fresh strawberries

1/2 cup rolled oats

1/2 cup Greek yogurt

A splash of vanilla extract

Sweetener as needed

Ice cubes

**Servings:** 1-2

**M.C.:** Blending

**Procedure:**

Blend strawberries, oats, Greek yogurt, vanilla extract, sweetener, and ice cubes until smooth.

Taste and adjust sweetness as necessary.

Serve in a tall glass, garnished with a strawberry on the rim for a smoothie that tastes like strawberry shortcake.

**N.V.:** Packed with vitamin C from strawberries, probiotics from Greek yogurt, and fiber from oats.

## Recipe 8: Banana Cream Pie Smoothie

**P.T.:** 5 minutes

**Ingr.:**

1 large ripe banana

1/2 cup Greek yogurt

1/4 teaspoon vanilla extract

1 tablespoon honey

1/2 cup ice cubes

**Servings:** 1-2

**M.C.:** Blending

**Procedure:**

Combine banana, Greek yogurt, vanilla extract, honey, and ice cubes in a blender.

Blend until creamy.

Serve with a sprinkle of crushed graham crackers on top for that pie crust effect.

**N.V.:** A dessert-like treat rich in potassium from the banana and protein from the Greek yogurt.

## Recipe 9: Carrot Cake Smoothie

**P.T.:** 5 minutes

**Ingr.:**

1/2 cup grated carrot

1/2 ripe banana

1/4 cup walnuts

A dash of cinnamon and nutmeg

1 cup almond milk

Sweetener if desired

**Servings:** 1-2

**M.C.:** Blending

**Procedure:**

Add grated carrot, banana, walnuts, spices, almond milk, and sweetener to a blender.

Blend until smooth.

Enjoy a smoothie that brings the flavors of carrot cake in a glass.

**N.V.:** Offers a good source of beta-carotene from carrots, omega-3 fatty acids from walnuts, and spices with anti-inflammatory properties.

### Recipe 10: Mojito-Inspired Minty Lime Smoothie

**P.T.:** 5 minutes

**Ingr.:**

Juice of 3 limes

1/2 cup fresh mint leaves

1 ripe avocado

1/2 cup ice

Sweetener to taste

**Servings:** 1-2

**M.C.:** Blending

**Procedure:**

Blend lime juice, mint leaves, avocado, ice, and sweetener in a blender until smooth.

Adjust sweetness as needed.

Serve in a chilled glass, garnished with mint leaves for a refreshing, dessert-inspired smoothie.

**N.V.:** Avocado provides healthy fats and fiber, lime and mint offer a refreshing zest and aid in digestion.

# 8. Fusion Juices: The Best of Both Worlds

## Fruit and Vegetable Blends

### Recipe 1: Sunrise Citrus Beet

**P.T.:** 10 minutes

**Ingr.:**

2 medium beets, peeled and chopped

2 oranges, peeled and quartered

1 carrot, peeled and chopped

1/2 inch ginger, peeled

Juice of 1 lemon

**Servings:** 2

**M.C.:** Juicing

**Procedure:**

Add beets, oranges, carrot, and ginger to the juicer.

Collect the juice in a large container, stirring in the lemon juice at the end.

Serve the juice immediately or chill for an hour before serving to enhance the flavors.

**N.V.:** High in vitamin C, potassium, and antioxidants. The ginger adds a spicy kick and aids digestion.

### Recipe 2: Green Pineapple Bliss

**P.T.:** 10 minutes

**Ingr.:**

1 cup spinach leaves

1/2 pineapple, peeled and cored

1 cucumber, chopped

1/2 avocado

Juice of 1 lime

**Servings:** 2

**M.C.:** Blending

**Procedure:**

Combine spinach, pineapple, cucumber, and avocado in a blender.

Add lime juice for a tangy flavor.

Blend until smooth, adding water if needed for the desired consistency.

Serve chilled for a refreshing, nutrient-packed drink.

**N.V.:** Loaded with vitamins A, C, and E, fiber, and healthy fats from avocado.

### Recipe 3: Carrot Apple Zinger

**P.T.:** 5 minutes

**Ingr.:**

3 large carrots, peeled

2 green apples, cored

1-inch piece of ginger, peeled

1/2 teaspoon ground turmeric

**Servings:** 2

**M.C.:** Juicing

**Procedure:**

Juice the carrots, apples, and ginger together, capturing their essence in a pitcher.

Stir in the ground turmeric for an additional anti-inflammatory boost.

Serve immediately, or chill for a refreshing and invigorating drink.

**N.V.:** This juice is a powerhouse of vitamins A and C, with ginger and turmeric providing digestive and anti-inflammatory benefits.

### Recipe 4: Berry Spinach Delight

**P.T.:** 5 minutes

**Ingr.:**

1 cup fresh spinach

1 cup mixed berries (strawberries, blueberries, raspberries), fresh or frozen

1 ripe banana

1/2 cup unsweetened almond milk

**Servings:** 2

**M.C.:** Blending

**Procedure:**

Add the spinach, mixed berries, banana, and almond milk to a blender.

Blend until smooth, adding more almond milk if needed to reach your preferred consistency.

Serve the smoothie immediately for a burst of antioxidants and a creamy, satisfying treat.

**N.V.:** Loaded with antioxidants, fiber, and essential minerals. The spinach provides iron while the berries offer a wealth of antioxidants.

### Recipe 5: Tropical Turmeric Cleanser

**P.T.:** 5 minutes

**Ingr.:**

1 cup pineapple chunks

1 cup mango chunks, fresh or frozen

1 medium carrot, peeled and chopped

1 teaspoon turmeric powder

1 cup coconut water

**Servings:** 2

**M.C.:** Blending

**Procedure:**

Combine pineapple, mango, carrot, turmeric powder, and coconut water in a blender.

Blend until smooth and vibrant in color.

Serve this tropical fusion juice immediately, enjoying the hydrating and anti-inflammatory benefits.

**N.V.:** High in vitamins A, C, and E, with turmeric adding a potent anti-inflammatory effect and coconut water ensuring hydration.

## Recipe 6: Cucumber Melon Hydrator

**P.T.:** 5 minutes

**Ingr.:**

1 large cucumber, chopped

2 cups honeydew melon, cubed

1/4 cup fresh mint leaves

Juice of 1 lime

**Servings:** 2

**M.C.:** Blending

**Procedure:**

Blend cucumber, honeydew melon, mint leaves, and lime juice until smooth.

Serve chilled for an ultra-refreshing and hydrating drink, perfect for hot summer days.

**N.V.:** Offers hydration and essential nutrients, including vitamin C and potassium, with mint providing digestive benefits.

## Recipe 7: Sweet Potato Sunrise

**P.T.:** 10 minutes

**Ingr.:**

1 medium sweet potato, cooked and cooled

2 oranges, peeled and segmented

1 carrot, peeled and chopped

A dash of cinnamon

1 cup water or orange juice

**Servings:** 2

**M.C.:** Blending

**Procedure:**

Combine the sweet potato, oranges, carrot, cinnamon, and water/orange juice in a blender.

Blend until smooth, adding more liquid if necessary to achieve desired consistency.

Serve immediately for a nutritious, energy-boosting start to your day.

**N.V.:** Rich in beta-carotene, vitamins C and A, and fiber. Cinnamon adds anti-inflammatory properties and balances blood sugar levels.

## Recipe 8: Beetroot Berry Fusion

**P.T.:** 5 minutes

**Ingr.:**

1 medium beetroot, peeled and chopped

1 cup strawberries

1 small apple, cored and sliced

A handful of kale leaves

1 cup water or vegetable juice

**Servings:** 2

**M.C.:** Blending

**Procedure:**

Place beetroot, strawberries, apple, kale, and water/vegetable juice into a blender.

Blend until smooth, adding more liquid if necessary for a pourable consistency.

Enjoy a nutrient-dense juice that combines the sweetness of fruit with the earthiness of beetroot and kale.

**N.V.:** A great source of antioxidants, fiber, and vitamins. Beetroot boosts stamina and improves blood flow.

### Recipe 9: Celery Pear Cleanse

**P.T.:** 5 minutes

**Ingr.:**

3 stalks of celery, chopped

1 ripe pear, cored and sliced

1 cup spinach

Juice of 1 lemon

1 cup cucumber, chopped

**Servings:** 2

**M.C.:** Blending

**Procedure:**

Combine celery, pear, spinach, lemon juice, and cucumber in a blender.

Blend until the mixture is smooth and evenly combined.

Serve chilled for a light, detoxifying drink that aids in digestion and refreshes the palate.

**N.V.:** Loaded with vitamins K and C, potassium, and water content for hydration and detoxification.

## Tropical Mixes

### Recipe 1: Mango Passion Fruit Bliss

**P.T.:** 5 minutes

**Ingr.:**

1 ripe mango, peeled and cubed

2 passion fruits, halved and scooped

1/2 cup coconut water

Juice of 1 lime

Ice cubes (optional)

**Servings:** 2

**M.C.:** Blending

**Procedure:**

Blend the mango, passion fruit pulp, coconut water, and lime juice until smooth.

If desired, add ice cubes to the blender for a chillier beverage.

Serve immediately, garnished with a slice of lime or a few mint leaves.

**N.V.:** High in vitamins A and C, antioxidants, and hydration properties. The lime juice adds a refreshing zesty flavor.

### Recipe 2: Pineapple Coconut Hydrator

**P.T.:** 5 minutes

**Ingr.:**

1 cup pineapple chunks

1 cup coconut milk

Juice of 1/2 orange

1/2 banana, for sweetness

A handful of ice cubes

**Servings:** 2

**M.C.:** Blending

**Procedure:**

Combine pineapple, coconut milk, orange juice, and banana in a blender.

Add ice cubes and blend until smooth and frothy.

Serve in tall glasses, perhaps with a sprinkle of grated coconut on top for an extra tropical touch.

**N.V.:** Offers a good source of vitamin C, manganese, and healthy fats. The banana provides additional potassium and fiber.

### Recipe 3: Kiwi Cucumber Cooler

**P.T.:** 5 minutes

**Ingr.:**

3 ripe kiwis, peeled and sliced

1 large cucumber, chopped

1/2 cup apple juice

A handful of fresh mint leaves

Ice cubes (optional)

**Servings:** 2

**M.C.:** Blending

**Procedure:**

In a blender, combine kiwis, cucumber, apple juice, and mint leaves.

Add ice cubes for a cooler beverage, if desired.

Blend until smooth and uniformly mixed.

Serve immediately, garnished with extra mint or kiwi slices for a refreshing and hydrating drink.

**N.V.:** Rich in vitamin C and antioxidants from kiwi, hydration from cucumber, and a minty freshness that aids digestion.

### Recipe 4: Tropical Turmeric Tonic

**P.T.:** 5 minutes

**Ingr.:**

1 inch turmeric root, peeled and chopped

1 cup pineapple chunks

1 cup mango chunks

Juice of 1 lemon

1 cup coconut water

**Servings:** 2

**M.C.:** Blending

**Procedure:**

Place turmeric, pineapple, mango, lemon juice, and coconut water in a blender.

Blend until the mixture is smooth and the turmeric is fully integrated.

Serve the juice immediately to enjoy its anti-inflammatory and immune-boosting benefits.

**N.V.:** Provides a potent anti-inflammatory boost from turmeric, hydration from coconut water, and vitamins A and C from mango and pineapple.

## Recipe 5: Caribbean Citrus Burst

**P.T.:** 5 minutes

**Ingr.:**

2 oranges, peeled and quartered

1 grapefruit, peeled and quartered

Juice of 2 limes

1/2 inch ginger, peeled

**Servings:** 2

**M.C.:** Juicing

**Procedure:**

Juice the oranges, grapefruit, limes, and ginger together.

Stir the juice well to ensure the flavors meld together.

Serve chilled for a zesty, vitamin C-rich drink that energizes and refreshes.

**N.V.:** High in vitamin C, antioxidants, and ginger provides digestive benefits.

## Recipe 6: Banana Berry Lagoon

**P.T.:** 5 minutes

Ingr.:

2 ripe bananas

1 cup mixed berries (fresh or frozen)

1 cup coconut milk

A dash of vanilla extract

Servings: 2

M.C.: Blending

Procedure:

Combine bananas, mixed berries, coconut milk, and vanilla extract in a blender.

Blend until creamy and smooth.

Pour into glasses and serve immediately for a sweet, creamy tropical treat.

**N.V.:** Loaded with fiber from bananas and berries, healthy fats from coconut milk, and a touch of natural sweetness.

## Recipe 7: Avocado Lime Smoothie

**P.T.:** 5 minutes

**Ingr.:**

1 ripe avocado

Juice of 2 limes

1 cup spinach leaves

2 tablespoons honey or to taste

1 cup water or coconut water

**Servings:** 2

**M.C.:** Blending

**Procedure:**

Scoop the avocado into a blender, adding lime juice, spinach, honey, and water/coconut water.

Blend until smooth and creamy.

Adjust sweetness with more honey if needed, and serve chilled for a nutrient-dense, creamy smoothie.

**N.V.:** High in healthy fats, vitamins K, C, E, and fiber. Lime adds a refreshing tang, and spinach boosts iron and calcium intake.

### Recipe 8: Papaya Ginger Sunrise

**P.T.:** 5 minutes

**Ingr.:**

1 cup papaya, cubed

1/2 cup carrot juice

1 small piece of ginger, peeled

Juice of 2 oranges

**Servings:** 2

**M.C.:** Blending

**Procedure:**

Blend papaya, carrot juice, ginger, and orange juice until smooth.

Serve immediately, enjoying the digestive benefits of ginger with the vitamins from papaya and carrot.

**N.V.:** A vibrant source of vitamins A, C, and E, with ginger adding digestive aid and anti-inflammatory properties.

### Recipe 9: Dragon Fruit Dream

**P.T.:** 5 minutes

**Ingr.:**

1 dragon fruit, peeled and cubed

2 kiwis, peeled and sliced

1 banana

1 cup almond milk

**Servings:** 2

**M.C.:** Blending

**Procedure:**

Add dragon fruit, kiwis, banana, and almond milk to a blender.

Blend until the mixture is smooth and has a vibrant pink color.

Serve chilled for a visually stunning and deliciously exotic smoothie.

**N.V.:** Full of antioxidants, vitamin C, and fiber. The almond milk provides a creamy texture without overwhelming the delicate flavors of the fruits.

energy.

# Antioxidant-Rich Combinations

## Recipe 1: Berry Beet Bliss

**P.T.:** 5 minutes

**Ingr.:**

1 medium beet, peeled and chopped

1 cup mixed berries (strawberries, blueberries, raspberries)

1 orange, peeled and segmented

1/2 inch piece of ginger, peeled

1 cup water or coconut water

**Servings:** 2

**M.C.:** Blending

**Procedure:**

Combine beet, mixed berries, orange segments, ginger, and water/coconut water in a blender.

Blend until smooth. If the mixture is too thick, add more water to achieve the desired consistency.

Strain through a fine mesh sieve for a smoother texture, if preferred.

Serve immediately or chilled, garnished with a berry or orange slice.

**N.V.:** High in antioxidants, vitamin C, and fiber. Ginger adds anti-inflammatory properties.

## Recipe 2: Green Tea Citrus Twist

**P.T.:** 10 minutes (including brewing time)

**Ingr.:**

1 cup brewed green tea, cooled

Juice of 1 lemon

Juice of 1 lime

1/2 cucumber, sliced

1 apple, cored and sliced

Honey or agave syrup to taste

**Servings:** 2

**M.C.:** Blending

**Procedure:**

Brew the green tea and allow it to cool.

In a blender, combine the cooled green tea, lemon and lime juices, cucumber, and apple.

Add honey or agave syrup to sweeten as desired.

Blend until smooth.

Serve immediately, offering a refreshing and antioxidant-rich beverage.

**N.V.:** Loaded with antioxidants from green tea and citrus, hydration from cucumber, and natural sweetness from apple.

## Recipe 3: Pomegranate Blueberry Punch

**P.T.:** 5 minutes

**Ingr.:**

1 cup pomegranate juice

1/2 cup blueberries, fresh or frozen

1 ripe banana

Splash of acai juice

Ice cubes, optional

**Servings:** 2

**M.C.:** Blending

**Procedure:**

Place the pomegranate juice, blueberries, banana, and acai juice in a blender.

Add ice cubes if a colder beverage is desired.

Blend until smooth and well combined.

Serve immediately, garnished with a few whole blueberries or a slice of lime for an extra touch.

**N.V.:** Loaded with antioxidants from pomegranate, blueberries, and acai. Bananas add potassium and fiber for a balanced drink.

## Recipe 4: Carrot Ginger Turmeric Elixir

**P.T.:** 10 minutes

**Ingr.:**

4 large carrots, peeled and chopped

1 inch piece of turmeric, peeled

1/2 inch piece of ginger, peeled

Juice of 2 oranges

Honey or agave syrup, to taste

**Servings:** 2

**M.C.:** Juicing/Blending

**Procedure:**

Juice carrots, turmeric, and ginger. If using a blender, add a little water to help blend smoothly then strain.

Stir in the orange juice and add honey or agave syrup to sweeten as needed.

Serve chilled for a vibrant, immune-boosting juice.

**N.V.:** High in vitamin A from carrots, anti-inflammatory properties from turmeric, and digestive benefits from ginger.

## Recipe 5: Spinach Kiwi Cooler

**P.T.:** 5 minutes

**Ingr.:**

2 cups fresh spinach leaves

2 ripe kiwis, peeled and sliced

1 green apple, cored and sliced

Juice of 1 lime

1/2 cup water or coconut water

**Servings:** 2

**M.C.:** Blending

**Procedure:**

Combine spinach, kiwis, apple, lime juice, and water/coconut water in a blender.

Blend until smooth, adding more liquid if needed for desired consistency.

Serve immediately for a refreshing and nutrient-packed green juice.

**N.V.:** Offers a rich source of vitamin C, vitamin K, dietary fiber, and antioxidants.

## Recipe 6: Watermelon Basil Quencher

**P.T.:** 5 minutes

**Ingr.:**

4 cups cubed watermelon

A handful of fresh basil leaves

Juice of 1 lime

Ice cubes, optional

**Servings:** 2-3

**M.C.:** Blending

**Procedure:**

Blend watermelon, basil leaves, and lime juice until smooth.

Add ice cubes for a slushier texture if desired.

Serve in tall glasses, garnished with basil leaves for a hydrating and refreshing drink.

**N.V.:** High in vitamins A and C, lycopene, and has anti-inflammatory properties from the basil.

### Recipe 7: Cranberry Apple Zest

**P.T.:** 5 minutes

**Ingr.:**

1 cup cranberry juice (unsweetened)

1 apple, cored and sliced

Dash of cinnamon

Juice of 1 lemon

Honey or agave syrup, to taste

**Servings:** 2

**M.C.:** Blending

**Procedure:**

Combine cranberry juice, apple slices, cinnamon, and lemon juice in a blender.

Add honey or agave syrup according to your sweetness preference.

Blend until smooth.

Serve chilled for a tart, antioxidant-rich beverage with a hint of spice.

**N.V.:** Cranberries are rich in antioxidants, apples provide dietary fiber, and cinnamon offers anti-inflammatory benefits.

### Recipe 8: Cherry Almond Antioxidant Smoothie

**P.T.:** 5 minutes

**Ingr.:**

1 cup cherries, pitted (fresh or frozen)

1 cup almond milk

1 tablespoon almond butter

A dash of vanilla extract

Honey or maple syrup, to taste

**Servings:** 2

**M.C.:** Blending

**Procedure:**

Place cherries, almond milk, almond butter, vanilla extract, and sweetener in a blender.

Blend until smooth and creamy.

Serve immediately, offering a heart-healthy, antioxidant-packed smoothie.

**N.V.:** Cherries provide antioxidants and anti-inflammatory compounds, almond milk and butter offer healthy fats and vitamin E.

### Recipe 9: Sweet Potato Sunrise

**P.T.:** 10 minutes

**Ingr.:**

1 medium sweet potato, cooked and cooled

Juice of 2 oranges

1 carrot, peeled and chopped

A dash of nutmeg

Water or orange juice, for blending

**Servings:** 2

**M.C.:** Blending

**Procedure:**

Blend sweet potato, orange juice, carrot, nutmeg, and a bit of water/orange juice until smooth.

Adjust the consistency with more liquid if needed.

Serve this beta-carotene-rich juice for a sweet, nutritious start to your day.

**N.V.:** Packed with vitamins A and C, fiber, and antioxidants. Nutmeg adds a warming note and aids digestion.

# Refreshing Hydration Juices

### Recipe 1: Cucumber Mint Refresher

**P.T.:** 5 minutes

**Ingr.:**

2 large cucumbers, chopped

A handful of fresh mint leaves

Juice of 1 lime

1 tablespoon honey (optional)

1 cup water or sparkling water

**Servings:** 2

**M.C.:** Blending

**Procedure:**

Combine cucumbers, mint leaves, lime juice, and honey in a blender. Add a cup of water for a smoother consistency.

Blend until smooth. For a more juice-like consistency, strain the mixture using a fine mesh sieve.

Serve over ice, topped with sparkling water for an extra refreshing touch.

**N.V.:** Rich in hydration from cucumber, vitamin C from lime, and with mint known for its digestive benefits.

### Recipe 2: Watermelon Basil Bliss

**P.T.:** 5 minutes

**Ingr.:**

4 cups cubed watermelon

A handful of fresh basil leaves

Juice of 1/2 lemon

Ice cubes

**Servings:** 2

**M.C.:** Blending

**Procedure:**

Add watermelon, basil leaves, and lemon juice to a blender.

Blend until smooth. For a chilled juice, add ice cubes directly to the blender or serve over ice.

Serve immediately, garnishing with extra basil leaves if desired.

**N.V.:** High in vitamins A and C from watermelon, with basil adding a unique flavor and lemon boosting detoxification.

### Recipe 3: Pineapple Coconut Hydrator

**P.T.:** 5 minutes

**Ingr.:**

2 cups fresh pineapple chunks

1 cup coconut water

Juice of 1 lime

Ice cubes (optional)

**Servings:** 2

**M.C.:** Blending

**Procedure:**

In a blender, combine pineapple chunks, coconut water, and lime juice.

Blend until smooth. For a cooler beverage, blend with ice cubes or serve over ice.

Serve garnished with a slice of pineapple or lime wedge for a tropical, hydrating treat.

**N.V.:** This drink is an excellent source of hydration and electrolytes from coconut water, vitamin C from pineapple, and a refreshing zest from lime.

### Recipe 4: Green Apple Hydration

**P.T.:** 5 minutes

**Ingr.:**

2 green apples, cored and sliced

3 stalks of celery

1/2 cucumber

A handful of kale leaves

1/2 cup water

**Servings:** 2

**M.C.:** Juicing

**Procedure:**

Pass the apples, celery, cucumber, and kale through a juicer.

Stir in water to dilute the juice to your liking. Serve immediately, possibly over ice, for a crisp and refreshing nutrient boost.

**N.V.:** Loaded with vitamins A, C, and K, plus minerals like potassium and magnesium for overall health and hydration.

### Recipe 5: Berry Citrus Splash

**P.T.:** 5 minutes

**Ingr.:**

1 cup strawberries

1/2 cup blueberries

Juice of 2 oranges

Juice of 1 lemon

Ice cubes

**Servings:** 2

**M.C.:** Blending

**Procedure:**

Blend strawberries, blueberries, orange juice, and lemon juice until smooth.

Add ice cubes to the blender for a chilled juice or serve over ice.

Pour into glasses and enjoy a vibrant, antioxidant-rich drink.

**N.V.:** High in antioxidants and vitamin C, supporting immune health and offering anti-inflammatory benefits.

## Recipe 6: Ginger Peach Quencher

**P.T.:** 5 minutes

**Ingr.:**

2 ripe peaches, pitted and sliced

1-inch piece of ginger, peeled

Juice of 1 lemon

1 cup water or sparkling water

Honey or agave syrup, to taste

**Servings:** 2

**M.C.:** Blending

**Procedure:**

Blend peaches, ginger, lemon juice, and water until smooth.

Sweeten with honey or agave syrup as desired.

Serve over ice or with a splash of sparkling water for a fizzy, refreshing twist.

**N.V.:** A perfect blend for digestion and nausea relief from ginger, with peaches adding sweetness and hydration.

## Recipe 7: Citrus Cucumber Cooler

**P.T.:** 5 minutes

**Ingr.:**

1 large cucumber, sliced

Juice of 1 grapefruit

Juice of 2 oranges

Juice of 1 lime

Mint leaves for garnish

**Servings:** 2

**M.C.:** Juicing/Blending

**Procedure:**

Juice or blend cucumber, grapefruit, oranges, and lime together.

If blended, strain for a smoother texture.

Serve chilled, garnished with mint leaves for a refreshing and detoxifying juice.

**N.V.:** Packed with vitamin C, hydration from cucumber, and liver detoxification support from grapefruit.

## Recipe 8: Melon Mint Medley

**P.T.:** 5 minutes

**Ingr.:**

2 cups cubed cantaloupe

2 cups cubed honeydew melon

A handful of fresh mint leaves

Juice of 1/2 lime

Ice cubes

**Servings:** 2

**M.C.:** Blending

**Procedure:**

Combine cantaloupe, honeydew melon, mint leaves, lime juice, and ice cubes in a blender.

Blend until smooth and frothy.

Serve immediately for a cooling and hydrating beverage.

**N.V.:** Offers hydration and essential nutrients like vitamins A and C, with mint providing a refreshing aftertaste.

### Recipe 9: Tropical Green Hydration

**P.T.:** 5 minutes

**Ingr.:**

1 cup spinach leaves

1 cup pineapple chunks

1 banana

1 cup coconut water

**Servings:** 2

**M.C.:** Blending

**Procedure:**

Place spinach, pineapple, banana, and coconut water into a blender.

Blend until smooth, adding more coconut water if needed.

Enjoy a tropical smoothie that's perfect for hydration and a nutrient boost.

**N.V.:** Rich in potassium from banana and coconut water, vitamins A and C from pineapple and spinach.

# 9. Your 21-Day Juice Cleanse

## Week 1

| Day | Breakfast | Lunch | Dinner |
|---|---|---|---|
| Monday | Oatmeal with sliced bananas and almonds | Grilled chicken salad with mixed greens, cherry tomatoes, and avocado | Baked salmon with steamed broccoli and quinoa |
| Tuesday | Greek yogurt with mixed berries and a drizzle of honey | Turkey and avocado wrap with whole wheat tortilla | Stir-fried tofu with mixed vegetables and brown rice |
| Wednesday | Scrambled eggs with spinach and whole-grain toast | Quinoa salad with black beans, corn, and diced peppers | Grilled shrimp over mixed greens with a lemon vinaigrette dressing |
| Thursday | Smoothie with spinach, banana, protein powder, and almond milk | Chicken Caesar salad with romaine lettuce and whole-grain croutons | Beef stir-fry with bell peppers, broccoli, and a side of jasmine rice |
| Friday | Whole-grain pancakes topped with fresh strawberries and a small amount of maple syrup | Lentil soup with a side of whole-grain bread | Baked cod with sweet potato mash and green beans |
| Saturday | Avocado toast on whole-grain bread with a side of cottage cheese | Tuna salad over mixed greens with cucumber and olives | Chicken fajitas with sautéed onions and peppers, served with whole-grain tortillas |
| Sunday | Omelet with mushrooms, onions, and feta cheese, with a side of fruit salad | Chickpea and vegetable curry served with basmati | Zucchini noodles (zoodles) with turkey meatballs and marinara |

| Day | Breakfast | Lunch | Dinner |
|---|---|---|---|
|  |  | rice | sauce |

## Week 2

| Day | Breakfast | Lunch | Dinner |
|---|---|---|---|
| Monday | Chia seed pudding with almond milk and mixed berries | Quinoa and roasted vegetable bowl with tahini dressing | Pan-seared trout with asparagus and wild rice |
| Tuesday | Whole-grain toast with peanut butter and sliced banana | Lentil and vegetable stew with a side of whole-grain bread | Turkey meatloaf with mashed cauliflower and steamed green beans |
| Wednesday | Cottage cheese with pineapple chunks and walnuts | Spinach and feta stuffed chicken breast with a side salad | Vegetarian chili with kidney beans, black beans, and corn, served with brown rice |
| Thursday | Smoothie bowl with kale, avocado, protein powder, topped with granola | Mediterranean chickpea salad with tomatoes, cucumbers, olives, and feta | Grilled lamb chops with mint sauce, roasted sweet potatoes, and Brussels sprouts |
| Friday | Scrambled tofu with turmeric, black pepper, onions, and tomatoes | Sardine salad with mixed greens, avocado, and whole-grain crackers | Baked chicken thighs with quinoa and roasted carrots |
| Saturday | Almond butter and jelly on whole-grain bread with a side of Greek yogurt | Beef and broccoli stir-fry with a side of jasmine rice | Spaghetti squash with homemade meat sauce and a side of garlic bread |
| Sunday | Baked sweet potato with cottage cheese and chives | Grilled vegetable and hummus wrap in a whole wheat tortilla | Pan-fried salmon with a dill yogurt sauce, quinoa, and sautéed |

The glossary would be incomplete without a nod to the superheroes of the juicing world—the phytonutrients. These natural compounds, with names as exotic as their origins—flavonoids, carotenoids, and glucosinolates—usher in a spectrum of health benefits, from anti-inflammatory prowess to cancer-fighting capabilities. They're the hidden gems in our glasses, offering protection and vitality with every sip. In the realm of juicing, the artistry lies in the symphony of flavors, the delicate balance between the sweet whispers of fruit and the earthy tones of vegetables. The acidity of citrus, the sweetness of apples, and the boldness of beets; each ingredient contributes its verse to the juice's song, creating a harmony that delights the palate and nourishes the body. Juicing is not just a culinary endeavor; it's a lifestyle, a testament to the abundance of nature and the body's innate wisdom. It invites us to explore, experiment, and engage with our food in its most elemental form. This glossary, then, is more than a collection of terms; it's a map to treasure, a guide to a world brimming with vitality, waiting to be discovered. In this exploration, examples abound, from the novice juicer marveling at the transformation of a simple carrot into a vibrant drink, to the seasoned aficionado crafting a blend that sings with complexity and depth. Each experience, each glass of juice, is a step on the path to wellness, a journey that nourishes the body, delights the senses, and honors the earth. So, as you embark on this journey, let the glossary be your guide, a companion in your exploration of the rich landscape of juicing. Let it inspire you to blend, to taste, to savor, and to thrive. For in the world of juicing, every ingredient, every term, and every drop of juice is a thread in the vibrant tapestry of health and vitality.

# Frequently Asked Questions

Embarking on a juicing journey is akin to navigating a vibrant landscape filled with the lushness of fruits and the verdancy of vegetables, each offering a cornucopia of health benefits and gustatory delights. As with any voyage into uncharted territories, questions arise, sparked by curiosity and a desire to delve deeper into the art and science of juicing. Here, we seek to illuminate the path, answering inquiries that bubble up from the wellspring of enthusiasm for transforming nature's bounty into liquid nourishment. Why do people juice? The essence of juicing lies not just in its ability to condense a multitude of vitamins, minerals, and phytonutrients into a single glass but also in its role as a beacon of wellness, guiding individuals towards a more vibrant state of health. Juicing is a celebration of life, extracting the vibrant essence of fruits and vegetables, and serving it in a form that the body can easily assimilate. It's a ritual that reconnects us with the natural world, reminding us of the simplicity of nourishment and the complexity of nature's nutritional tapestry. Can juicing replace eating whole fruits and vegetables? While juicing delivers a concentrated burst of nutrients and enzymes, it is not a substitute for the holistic benefits of consuming whole fruits and vegetables. The act of juicing removes fiber, a crucial element for digestive health, satiety, and blood sugar regulation. Thus, juicing should be viewed as a complement to a balanced diet, a liquid symphony that plays alongside the solid foods in the orchestra of our daily meals. What is the best time to drink juice? The answer whispers through the leaves of logic and intuition—consume juice when your body can best absorb the nutrients and when it aligns with your personal rhythms. Morning, with its fresh slate and empty stomach, presents an ideal canvas for the vibrant hues of juice, allowing the body to readily absorb the nutrients. However, the melody of life plays differently for each individual, and some may find a midday juice uplifts them, while others prefer a liquid feast as an evening elixir. How long does fresh juice retain its nutrients? The vitality of fresh juice ebbs with time, as exposure to air and light catalyzes the oxidation process, gradually diminishing the nutrient density and enzymatic activity. To capture the essence in its prime, it is advisable to drink juice immediately after its creation. However, when stored in an airtight container and refrigerated, most juices can maintain a significant portion of their nutritional orchestra for up to 24 hours, allowing you to savor the symphony a bit longer. Is it better to juice or blend? This question dances on the palate of personal preference and nutritional objectives. Juicing offers a concentrated nutrient infusion, a direct line to the bloodstream without the fiber to slow absorption. Blending, however, retains the fiber, crafting a smoothie that can act as a meal replacement or a fiber-rich treat.

Both methods have their place in the dietary landscape, serving different roles but united in their mission to nourish and revitalize. As we peel back the layers of curiosity, it becomes evident that juicing is more than a culinary trend; it is a gateway to a deeper understanding of nutrition and wellness, a tool that empowers individuals to take an active role in their health journey. Each question asked and answered is a step closer to unraveling the mysteries of nature's bounty, guiding us through a garden of possibilities where every fruit and vegetable holds the potential to nourish, heal, and delight.

# Resource Guide

In the verdant world of juicing, where the essence of nature's bounty is distilled into vibrant elixirs, the journey from novice to aficionado is an adventure filled with discovery, experimentation, and growth. To navigate this journey, a resource guide becomes an indispensable compass, pointing towards tools, ingredients, and wisdom that enrich the juicing experience, making each glass not just a drink, but a story of health, vitality, and connection to the earth. At the core of this adventure is the selection of a juicer, the alchemist's tool that transforms solid into liquid, fiber into juice. But the choice isn't merely about functionality; it's about finding a companion for your journey. Consider the centrifugal juicer, swift and efficient, ideal for the busy individual seeking nourishment amidst the whirlwind of daily life. Or the masticating juicer, slow and thorough, for the contemplative soul who sees juicing as a meditative ritual, savoring the richness of flavors and nutrients extracted at a deliberate pace. The quest for ingredients is a voyage in itself, a foray into the markets and farms where produce is not just food, but the culmination of sunlight, soil, and care. Here, the organic and the local aren't just labels, but stories of cultivation, of food raised without the shadow of chemicals, carrying the essence of the place it comes from. These markets become sanctuaries, spaces where choosing a kale leaf or a ripe tomato is a dialogue with the growers, a moment to learn and appreciate the journey of food from seed to store. Beyond the tangible—juicers and produce—lies the realm of knowledge, a vast ocean of recipes, techniques, and nutritional insights. Books and blogs authored by seasoned juicers offer maps to navigate this ocean, guiding through the mists of uncertainty and into harbors of understanding. Websites become lighthouses, shining light on the science of nutrition, the art of flavor combination, and the craft of juice preparation, illuminating paths towards health and wellness that extend well beyond the glass. Social media platforms and forums buzz with the conversations of a global community of juicers, a fellowship where questions are answered, experiences shared, and encouragement freely given. Here, in the digital agora, beginners find mentors, enthusiasts discover peers, and every post or comment weaves a stronger bond between individuals united by a common passion for juicing. But perhaps the most profound resources are the internal ones: curiosity, patience, and a willingness to experiment. These qualities unlock the true potential of juicing, transforming it from a mere dietary habit into a journey of self-discovery and wellness. They encourage to venture beyond familiar tastes into the realm of the exotic, to blend not just ingredients, but traditions and cultures, creating juices that are as diverse and vibrant as the world itself. In this resource guide, every tool, every ingredient, and every piece of knowledge is a thread in the tapestry of your juicing journey. Together, they form a picture not just of a dietary choice, but of a lifestyle that embraces health, respects nature, and celebrates the infinite variety and possibility contained within a single glass of juice.

# Index

The crafting of an index in a tome dedicated to the art and science of juicing is akin to laying down the final piece in a mosaic of knowledge. This intricate array, composed of myriad tiny, yet significant, fragments, forms a complete picture only when each part is meticulously placed in relation to the others. The index is not merely a tool; it's a bridge connecting the seeker of wisdom to the precise knowledge they require at any given moment. In the realm of juicing, where the vibrancy of nature is captured in every glass, the index serves as a lighthouse, guiding enthusiasts through the rich tapestry of content that makes up this comprehensive guide. It illuminates the path to understanding, ensuring that no question remains unanswered, no curiosity unfulfilled. Whether you're a novice embarking on your first juicing voyage or an experienced juicer seeking deeper insights into the nutritional nuances of your favorite concoctions, the index stands ready to direct you to the information you need. Navigating through topics as diverse as the nutritional breakdown of kale, the best methods for juicing a pomegranate, or the history of juicing across cultures, the index offers a structured panorama of the juicing universe. It respects the reader's time and thirst for knowledge by providing a straightforward pathway to the desired destination, be it a recipe for a sunrise citrus beet cleanse or an explanation of the enzymatic activity in fresh pineapple juice. In essence, the index is the silent guardian of the book's wisdom, a custodian of the secrets held within its pages. It invites exploration, promising that within the structure of entries, lie hidden gems waiting to be discovered. Through its organization, it speaks of the care and consideration woven into the fabric of the guide, reflecting a commitment to accessibility, understanding, and the joy of discovery. Thus, as we consider the index, we see more than a list. We see a commitment to the journey of health and wellness through juicing, an ode to the beauty of organized knowledge, and a testament to the transformative power of nature's bounty. It stands as the final note in a symphony of information, resonating with the promise of guidance, insight, and inspiration for all who seek to traverse the verdant landscapes of juicing.

# Measurement Conversion Table

## Volume Conversions

| Volume (Liquid) | US Customary Units | Metric Units |
|---|---|---|
| 1 teaspoon | 1 tsp | 5 milliliters (ml) |
| 1 tablespoon | 1 tbsp | 15 milliliters |
| 1 fluid ounce | 1 fl oz | 30 milliliters |
| 1 cup | 1 cup | 240 milliliters |
| 1 pint | 1 pt | 473 milliliters |
| 1 quart | 1 qt | 946 milliliters |
| 1 gallon | 1 gal | 3.785 liters |

## Weight Conversions

| Weight | US Customary Units | Metric Units |
|---|---|---|
| 1 ounce | 1 oz | 28 grams (g) |
| 1 pound | 1 lb | 454 grams |
| 1 kilogram | 2.2 lbs | 1000 grams (1 kg) |

## Length Conversions

| Length | US Customary Units | Metric Units |
|---|---|---|
| 1 inch | 1 in | 2.54 centimeters (cm) |
| 1 foot | 1 ft | 30.48 centimeters |

## Metric Volume Conversions

| Volume | Metric Units | US Customary Units |
|---|---|---|
| 1 milliliter (ml) | 1 ml | 0.034 fluid ounce (fl oz) |
| 100 milliliters | 100 ml | 3.4 fluid ounces |

| Volume      | Metric Units | US Customary Units |
|-------------|--------------|--------------------|
| 1 liter (L) | 1 L          | 34 fluid ounces    |
|             |              | 4.2 cups           |
|             |              | 2.1 pints          |
|             |              | 1.06 quarts        |
|             |              | 0.26 gallon        |

## Metric Weight Conversions

| Weight        | Metric Units | US Customary Units |
|---------------|--------------|--------------------|
| 1 gram (g)    | 1 g          | 0.035 ounces (oz)  |
| 100 grams     | 100 g        | 3.5 ounces         |
| 500 grams     | 500 g        | 1.1 pounds (lb)    |
| 1 kilogram (kg) | 1 kg       | 2.2 pounds         |

## Temperature Conversions

| Temperature      | Celsius (°C) | Fahrenheit (°F) |
|------------------|--------------|-----------------|
| Freezing Point   | 0°C          | 32°F            |
| Refrigerator     | 4°C          | 39°F            |
| Room Temperature | 20°C - 22°C  | 68°F - 72°F     |
| Boiling Water    | 100°C        | 212°F           |

Made in United States
Troutdale, OR
08/02/2024